What the Qur'an Meant

ALSO BY GARRY WILLS

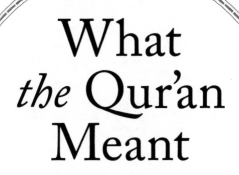

What
the Qur'an
Meant

And Why
It Matters

GARRY WILLS

VIKING

VIKING
An imprint of Penguin Random House LLC
375 Hudson Street
New York, New York 10014
penguin.com

Excerpts from *The Qur'an*, translated by M. A. S. Abdel Haleem, Oxford World Classics (2008). By permission of Oxford University Press.

LIBRARY OF CONGRESS CATALOGING-IN-PUBLICATION DATA
Name: Wills, Garry, 1934– author.
Title: What the Qur'an meant and why it matters / Garry Wills.
Description: New York : Viking, 2017. | Includes index.
Identifiers: LCCN 2017025971 (print) | LCCN 2017025389 (ebook) |
ISBN 9781101981023 (hardcover) | ISBN 9781101981030 (ebook)
Subjects: LCSH: Qur'an—Criticism, interpretation, etc. | Islam—Doctrines.
Classification: LCC BP130 .W55 2017 (ebook) | LCC BP130 (print) |
DDC 297.1/226—dc23
LC record available at https://lccn.loc.gov/2017025971

Printed in the United States of America
1   3   5   7   9   10   8   6   4   2

Set in Adobe Caslon Pro
Designed by Daniel Lagin

To Bud Moynihan
carissime

Contents

What the Qur'an Meant

Introduction:
My Qur'an Problem

Knowing something about the Qur'an might, in another time, have been an ornament of the moderately learned. Not now. Now we face a world where knowledge about the Qur'an must deal with militant misuses of it and blatantly distorted reports of what it says. To help the majority of believers in Islam, and to be helped by them, we must see how far terrorists have departed from the book they say they believe in.

Influential people in our country tell us blatant lies about the religion that is followed by millions of peaceful Muslims, and we have no way to correct those claims unless we look at the morality of the Qur'an.

Yet there are many people who would block our reading of it. They think the Qur'an is not for reading but for burning. A cranky southern pastor put the book on trial for crimes against humanity, and condemned it to the flames, with terrible consequences abroad.[1] It is a bit unfair to put a book on trial without reading it. William F. Buckley, Jr., had a more genteel punishment for the book—it should be banned from schools, lest children read it. Why? Because it inspired the Muslims of 9/11 to kill people "innocent of any infidelity this side of not adhering to it."[2] Presumably, it could inflame children to burn down their schools.

Mr. Buckley was hardly alone in blaming the Qur'an (which he clearly had not read) for the attacks of 9/11. Donald Trump was believed by his devotees when he claimed that he saw, that day, "thousands and thousands" of Muslims in Jersey City "cheering as that building was coming down."[3] When Jersey City police and reporters were unable to find any trace of such a gathering, Mr. Trump claimed that he saw it on TV, though no one could find a TV record of the fact. Trump's real gift was for intuiting what many people wanted to believe, and for serving that desire. A Reuters/Ipsos poll in the summer of 2016 found that 78 percent of Trump supporters thought that Islam was more likely than other religions to encourage terrorist acts.[4]

Actually, a range of polls around the world found a majority of Muslims opposed to the World Trade Center attack and other forms of violence. One extensive world poll by the Gallup organization found that 93 percent of Muslims opposed the 9/11 attacks.[5] After the 2005 terrorist bombings in London, a YouGov poll for the *Daily Telegraph* found only 6 percent of British Muslims fully approved of those attacks, while 88 percent did not approve.[6] Of course, as the noted Islamist scholar Patricia Crone points out, the approval of Muslim aggression is greater in countries where there is a majority-Muslim population than in countries (like the United States or the United Kingdom) where Muslims are a minority.[7] But a Pew poll found that even in majority-Muslim countries most Muslims oppose terrorist acts (like suicide bombings).[8]

More important, perhaps, is the fact that the Muslim majority that disapproves of terrorism is more religious (more Qur'an-based) than the minority that approves of terrorism—the latter act more on secular motives like resentment of colonial powers. Indeed, Patricia Crone notes that terrorists are theologically illiterate:

People like Osama bin Laden and Ayman al-Zawahiri don't even seem to know their own tradition all that well. Rather, they have stripped Islam of practically everything that most Muslims consider to be their religion.[9]

Thus, when ISIS claimed to be acting from the Qur'an, over 120 Muslim scholars denounced this as a perversion of the sacred text.[10] Many Muslim spiritual leaders deny that the Qur'an allows or blesses terrorism—38 of them signed a document of the Islamic Supreme Council of Canada, saying that no believer in the Qur'an may join the Islamic State or claim that its efforts are a legitimate jihad.[11] An edict saying the same thing was signed by 70,000 Muslim clerics in India.[12] Similar edicts have been issued in Spain, Egypt, and elsewhere.[13]

It is not only Muslim authorities who say that the Qur'an does not favor violence rather than peace. This is also a judgment about the book reached by studious non-Muslims—from a secularist genius like Edward Gibbon to a deeply pious man like Pope Francis. Gibbon wrote in the eighteenth century:

A pernicious tenet has been imputed to the Mahometans, the duty of extirpating all other religions by the sword. This charge of ignorance and bigotry is refuted by the Koran, by the history of the Musulman conquerors, and by their public and legal tolerations of the Christian worship.[14]

And Pope Francis wrote in the twenty-first century:

Authentic Islam and the proper reading of the Koran are opposed to every form of violence.[15]

Yet despite this mountain of evidence that the religion of Islam favors peace over violence, and the evidence of the vast majority of

Muslims who live as useful citizens in our midst (some of them, like Captain Humayun Khan, dying heroically in the United States Army), there is a large and lucrative business for telling Americans what horrible things are in the Qur'an (they aren't).[16] Dozens of states have passed or proposed bans on Shari'ah law, as if that were an evil product of the Qur'an (it isn't). Women with hijabs are considered dangerous, since they are clothing themselves according to the Qur'an (they are not). Men wearing turbans are shunned as Muslims (they are Sikhs). Mosques are being banned or defaced for teaching the Qur'an.

This is a dangerous way to alienate the vast numbers of Muslims in the world. Jointly, the two greatest bodies of religious believers, Christianity and Islam, represent over half of the inhabitants of our globe—2.2 billion Christians (31 percent of the population), 1.6 billion Muslims (23 percent of the population). By 2050 the numbers will be roughly equal.[17] Yet in this shrinking and interconnected world, there is a vast ignorance of Islam, its varieties, its hopeful possibilities and its lurking dangers. This ignorance undermines any sensible policies toward the Islamic world. The invasion of Iraq, for instance, the worst foreign policy decision of our recent history, was led by President Bush with no awareness that we were not just unseating a dictator but overthrowing a Sunni Muslim regime that ruled a Shia Muslim majority population, with predictable Sunni reprisals that continue to detonate.

I am unfortunately well qualified to speak about our ignorance where Muslims are concerned. After our disastrous invasion of Iraq, I was asked by a friend if I had ever read the Qur'an. I was embarrassed to answer her, "No." I had spent my whole adult life studying Christianity in one way or another, while remaining ignorant of the only other religion of a similar scale. And I was not alone in my ignorance. When I began to ask university audiences how many had read the Qur'an, dispiritingly few hands went up.

I have to admit that the Qur'an is not at first a gripping read. My early slogs through it were dutiful and apparently unrewarding. There are no obvious threads to follow, no apparent organizing principle. It is a series of disjunct revelations made to Muhammad, as recorded by his followers on pottery shards or other handy surfaces. These were transferred to paper, then arranged by believers after Muhammad's death, not in chronological or topical order but, *faute de mieux*, according to length (longer ones earlier, shorter ones toward the end).

Apart from the lack of an organizing outline, I found it difficult—without a constant teasing out of context—to know who is saying what to whom. The originating voice is Allah's (God's). But sometimes it is conveyed through Jibrail (the angel Gabriel); sometimes it is Allah speaking directly to Muhammad about his own life and family; but more frequently it is Muhammad passing Allah's message on to his fellow worshippers. At rare times, some new and unidentified voice seems to join the mix (e.g., 33.22, 66.4–5). The message is often what "We" teach or demand—but is that "We" Allah and Jibrail, Allah and Muhammad, or just Allah using the royal "We"?

The titles given to chapters—surahs—are not helpful. As often in oral cultures, they can refer to a catchword in the surah, or an oddity there, not the surah's main theme (when there is one) or principal event. "The Ants" is the title of Surah 27, not because that is the subject of the chapter, but because it is odd enough to be a hook for calling up a memory of it. The book, long as it is, is made for memorizing.

Some things in the book are off-putting—slavery, patriarchal attitudes toward women, religious militarism. But the same can be said of the biblical Torah. Muhammad was leading a minority group worshipping the One God, Allah, against many believers in many gods. He was upholding a new and an embattled cause, just as ancient Jews upheld the worship of the One God, Yahweh, against many idols and their devotees. There are peaceful Qur'an passages (mainly the revelations first begun in Mecca) and warlike passages (mainly revelations continued in the Prophet's displaced base of Medina)—just as there are pacific and bellicose counsels in the Torah. Allah, like Yahweh, is "a jealous God."

Despite these obstacles to easy reading, I felt it my duty (and that of others who shared my ignorance) to make what I could of a book so important to so many of our fellow humans on this earth. So I kept at it, however often I bogged down. I found my first way to fix my attention to the disparate surahs drifting off in what seemed different directions. From the outset I recognized in the book variations on stories I already knew—of the first man and woman and their fall from divine favor, or accounts of Noah's flood, of Moses's passage through the Red Sea, of Shaytan (Satan, also called Iblis) as a fallen jinni, and many others. These stories intrigued me by their twists on the familiar (as in a funhouse mirror).

I should not have found this surprising. There are many more prophets than Muhammad in the Qur'an: Abraham, Aaron, Ishmael, Isaac, Jacob, Joseph, Job, Lot, Jonah, Solomon, David, John (called Baptist in the New Testament), Jesus, and others. These familiar names and stories gave me a way to probe around in otherwise unfamiliar territory. As a kind of game at first, I marked O in the left margin for some parallel in the Old Testament and N in the right margin for the New Testament. Often, of course, the same passages got a double marking; but the ones with only an N made me, as a Catholic, feel at home. Like my fellow believers, Muslims honor Mary, the mother of Jesus. They believe in her perpetual virginity and sinlessness. She is the most honored woman in the

Qur'an—indeed, she is the only woman named in the book. Muslims believe that John the Baptist was miraculously born to be the forerunner of Jesus. They believe that Jesus was a great prophet who worked miracles, was led by a holy spirit, and was taken up to heaven. The Qur'an, like the Catholic catechism, proclaims belief in angels and devils, in heaven and hell, and in a Last Judgment that assigns people to their permanent place in eternity.

But after my attention was drawn to things I had some acquaintance with, I began to notice other things that intrigued me and drew me back to them—things like the book's pervasive sense of a desert culture, or the voicing of a dialogue with nature that is the way Allah communicates with his creatures, or the way every prophet's message is linked to every other prophet's message, or the casting of spiritual transactions in commercial imagery, or the various ways some women found to oppose patriarchal oppression. I began to see how people draw spiritual sustenance from the text, which is what Pope Francis praised in the Qur'an.[18] Those are the things I mean to explore in this book.

I did not find things I had been told to expect in the Qur'an. Where, for instance, were the seventy-two virgins who were supposed to be greeting the murderers of 9/11? They are not in the Qur'an at all, and are only in some discredited *ahadith* (traditions).[19] The unholy 9/11 crew—which practiced for their quite un-Muslim deeds by drinking and getting lap dances on earth—were quite ignorant of Islamic teachings.

Well, then, what did the scripture of Islam tell me about the duty to kill infidels? Some people are sure it is there, though it isn't. Then what does it say about Shari'ah law? Not a thing. The word *shari'ah* is used only once in the Qur'an, and not as a legal term. In Surah 45.18, Allah tells Muhammad that *he* (Muhammad) has been placed on a "clear path" (shari'ah), undistracted by other considerations—it is one of the many places where Allah assures or comforts the Prophet over the work he is assigning him. From this sole use of the word, I wonder how my fellow citizens come to know so much about Shari'ah—and know it they must, since in state after state of our republic they have outlawed, or taken steps to outlaw, what they are convinced is the menace of Shari'ah law.[20]

Over and over, actual acquaintance with the Qur'an failed to help me deal with Islam as other people perceive it. Did it make me understand the fatwa against Salman Rushdie? Or the *Charlie Hebdo* murders in Paris, the mass murders in San Bernardino? I had to confess that it told me nothing about those matters. I could not find in the Qur'an any definition of Shari'ah law, any defense of killing the innocent, any doctrine of fatwa. What good was reading the Qur'an, then, when it seems to have no relation to the major problems with Islam in our time, in our world?

That argument clearly has force. To cope with it, I tried to imagine myself completely ignorant of Christianity and going to that religion's source-document, the four Gospels of the New Testament. I might experience a sense of wonder on first encountering such strange stories, enough to make me feel, as I went away from them, as if I were walking in a newer and fresher world. But then I could be asked: What do those four accounts of the life of Jesus have to do with the Inquisition, with the Crusades, with Christians killing infidels, with Christians killing Christians? Or, to bring the questions into a more timely and modest focus for Americans, what do they have to do with outlawing homosexuality, abortion, contraception, pornography? If I answer (what is the entire truth) that there is nothing about any of those subjects in the Gospels, I could be dismissed as having undertaken a useless labor in reading documents that Christians no longer live by.

Still, I wonder what other method one might follow in studying a foreign religion. Should I begin with current or historic practices, and try to reason back from them toward some originally revealed teaching? That would call for long and tangled labors, since both Christianity and Islam have moved through historic eras that affected them in multiple ways. Believers in both began as a persecuted minority, then achieved some power—at first for self-defense, then for rule, then for empire. Believers in both religions have committed atrocities. Both have had times of reformation and of enlightenment. Both have had internecine wars against their own heretics, and separate ways of honoring their past, splintering that past into competing versions. When we speak of Christians, do we mean Catholics, Protestants, Eastern Orthodox, Pentecostals, Mormons, Quakers, Amish, Christian Scientists, or subgroups in all of these, or some amalgam of them all recognizable to few of them (if any)? Are we talking about Jerry Falwell or Dorothy Day? When we speak of Muslims, do we mean Shia, Sunni, Salafis, Sufis, Alawis, or subgroups in all of these, or some mix made of them by outside observers? How are we to sort out all these elements in the labyrinthine twistings of the two religions' separate/parallel histories?

There is still good reason to organize the search by beginning with what all these separate believers begin with, the Gospels in one case, the Qur'an in the other. Believers profess that these books are the sources and guides of their faith. From them they learn about Jesus or Muhammad. Neither of these founding figures wrote anything himself. In fact, Muslims argue that the words taken down from Allah (by way of Gabriel) could not have been written by Muhammad, since he was illiterate (62.6). As Allah tells Muhammad at Surah 29.48:

> You never recited any Scripture before We revealed this one to you; you never wrote one down with your hand. If you had done so, those who follow falsehood might have had cause to doubt.

Muhammad was sent to the unlettered, as one of them (7.157–58)—just as, in the past, the Gospels were thought to have been recorded by simple uneducated fishermen and other artisans. No one thinks Jesus or Muhammad could have earned (or wanted) a Ph.D.

The oral traditions about Jesus and Muhammad did not take the forms we know for several decades after their death. Yet both religions read these canonized sacred texts at their prayer services to this day. If their actions depart from the founding documents, it is not for lack of knowing the documents. Both religions call, at every turn in their history, for judgment in terms of the founding documents. How they justify any departure from the sources is bound to be a fascinating study. But we can only begin to measure these divergences by looking closely at their starting points—at the Gospels or the Qur'an.

So, even though my own effort at knowing about Islam begins in ignorance and must labor forward from that, the effort seems more useful than trying to generalize what Islam is from, for instance, the violence of the Islamic State, which has been called untrue to the faith by over 120 scholars of that faith, who themselves quote the Qur'an. We should not, in other words, take the destruction of the World Trade Center as expressing the essence of Islam, when an overwhelming majority of Muslims did not approve of that act (except in Donald Trump's lively imagination). We should not let our own extremists define Islam solely in terms of their extremists—which is not only an unjust but a dangerous course of action. It turns potential allies into enemies; it makes our own bellicosity push people away from us before they can explain themselves to us. Why force a large and diverse body of believers into a cramped space we define as its essence?

The tendency to generalize what Islam is from particular acts of particular Muslims is apparent in the outlawing of Shari'ah law before we even know what Shari'ah is, whether it comes in many varieties, how strictly or how widely it is observed among Muslims; whether it is in the Qur'an or derived from it; and whether it is derived validly or mistakenly. There are as many different attitudes toward it in Muslim populations as there are to Halakha among Jews both inside and outside of Israel (see chapter 9). Swiftly equating Shari'ah with the beheadings filmed by the Islamic State will not even alert us to the dangers that do lurk in some forms of Shari'ah. These attitudes reduce a rich long legal history to the passion of Lewis Carroll's Red Queen "stamping about, and shouting 'Off with his head!' or 'Off with her head!' about once in a minute."

Cognate with the determination to act against Shari'ah before determining where and how it is observed is the determination *not* to know the Qur'an or let others know about it, perpetuating for others my own beginner's ignorance of the book. Even to know or quote it is offensive to some, and a sign that one is (or is becoming) a Muslim—as if only Muslims can be allowed to know or quote the famous and influential book. When, in his Cairo speech of 2009, President Obama quoted the Qur'an (a thing even Pope Francis does), that was used by right-wing commentators to show that he is really a Muslim himself.

The willed ignorance of our anti-Muslims is met with a symmetrical ignorance from some Muslim countries. In America, the respected Christian evangelical school Wheaton College negotiated a professor, Larycia Hawkins, out of her tenure because she said online, "As Pope Francis stated, we worship the same God" (as Muslims do).[21] At Wheaton, only the Christian God is the real God. On the other side, in Malaysia, God answers to only one title, Allah, and Christians cannot use the name, even though the Malay-language Christian Bible had always used Allah as the word for God. When the Roman Catholic newsletter, the *Herald,* did what

Professor Hawkins did in Illinois—used Allah as the title for its God—it won a temporary court ruling in its favor (later overturned); ten Catholic churches were vandalized and one was gutted by fire.[22] This resembles the vandalizing of mosques in the United States. Some of us, on both sides, do not want to recognize the legitimacy of different religions in our midst.

But we must. We have already paid a terrible price for our ignorance about the people into whose lives we blundered in a "preemptive" war, the longest in our history and one that is still going on. We simply cannot afford to be so blind in a world as interdependent as our globe has become. There are three kinds of ignorance that cripple or undermine our ability to act intelligently when dealing with Islam as a religion, to identify distortions of that religion, and to strengthen our bonds with the peaceful Muslims in opposing distortions of that (or our) religion. The three are:

1. Secular ignorance, which made us blunder into Iraq thinking we could turn it into a democratic Disney World.
2. Religious ignorance, which pits our crusaders against their jihadists.
3. Fearful ignorance, which makes us think Muslims are infiltrating our government and national life.

But is it necessary to read the Qur'an in order to overcome these self-inflicted ignorances? What better start is there to understanding Islam as religion? That does not mean that all of us have to read it. But some of us do, and those who do must begin to outnumber those who attribute all kinds of falsehoods to the book. We do not need to become Islamic scholars to acquire a working knowledge of the religion as practiced by a quarter of the world.

I am not a Qur'an scholar, obviously. I cannot be one, since I do not know Arabic. Yet most of us, with differing degrees of adequacy, discuss Judaism without knowing the Hebrew of the Bible, or we discuss Christianity without knowing the Greek of the New Testament. That does not mean we can substitute our knowledge for that of the scholars. We have to listen to the scholars in order to maintain the level of what we do know about each other's views of important matters related to religion. This book is not a disquisition, it is a conversation—or the opening of one. After attempting to clear a space by reducing the three forms of ignorance that have been holding us back from understanding Islam, I shall explore what I have been able to learn and appreciate about the Qur'an.

This is not a model for others' reading of it. It is affected by my familiarity with one form of religious sensibility—my Roman Catholicism. Others can and should read it through their own particular lenses. That way I shall learn from differing approaches not confined to my own. The book invites this kind of exchange. If one wants scholarship, he or she should begin learning Arabic. Then go instantly to the admirable 1,988 pages of *The Study Quran* by Seyyed Hossein Nasr, Caner K. Dagli, Maria Massi Dakake, Joseph E. B. Lumbard, and Mohammed Rustom.[23] I use that book often, referred to henceforth as SQ. I consult other translations of the Qur'an, too, but for uniform convenience work from the standard Oxford rendering by Muhammad Abdel Haleem, referred to henceforth in parentheses by chapter and verse (surah and aya).*[24] In short:

Must we read the Qur'an?

We'd better.

---

* In quotations from the Qur'an, bracketed insertions in roman type are by Haleem. Bracketed insertions in *italic* type are by the author of this book.

NOTES

1. "Florida Preacher Burns Koran in Bizarre 'Trial and Execution' in Front of a Crowd of . . . 30 People," *Daily Mail*, Mar. 21, 2011. Enayat Najifizada and Rod Nordland, "Afghans Avenge Florida Koran Burning, Killing 12," *New York Times*, Apr. 1, 2011.
2. William F. Buckley, Jr., "Are We Owed an Apology?," Universal Press Syndicate, Aug. 19, 2002. People less sophisticated than Buckley were also trying to protect children's minds from the taint of knowing the Qur'an. A mother in Tennessee objected to her daughter's being taught the Qur'an in the seventh grade. She was applauded when she said, at a school board meeting, that "we must take back our families, schools, and our country." Apparently knowing something about the Qur'an robs us of our country. See Rick Wagner, "School Board Member Calls for Removal of Textbook over Islam Content," *Kingsport (Tennessee) Times-News*, Oct. 4, 2016.
3. Jim Dwyer, "Trump Refuted with Authority on 9/11 Claim," *New York Times*, Nov. 25, 2015.
4. Emily Flitter and Chris Kahn, "Republicans, Democrats Sharply Divided over Muslims in America," Reuters/Ipsos, July 15, 2016.
5. See the book written about the survey: John L. Esposito and Dalia Mogahed, *Who Speaks for Islam? What a Billion Muslims Really Think* (Gallup Press, 2007).
6. Anthony King, "One in Four Muslims Sympathises with the Motives of Terrorists," *Daily Telegraph*, July 23, 2005.
7. Patricia Crone, "Jihad and History," *openDemocracy*, July 30, 2007, p. 7.
8. "The Great Divide: How Westerners and Muslims View Each Other," Pew Global Attitudes Project, June 22, 2006.
9. Crone, op. cit., p. 7.
10. "Open Letter to Al-Baghdadi," Sept. 19, 2014.
11. "Historic Islamic Edict (Fatwa) on Joining ISIL/ISIS," ISCC, Mar. 11, 2015.
12. Caroline Mortimer, "70,000 Indian Muslim Clerics Issue Fatwa Against ISIS, the Taliban, al-Qaeda and Other Terror Groups," *Independent* (London), Dec. 10, 2015.
13. See, for instance, the edict endorsed by Al-Azhar University of Cairo: Muhammad Tahir-ul-Qadri, *Fatwa on Terrorism and Suicide Bombings* (Minhaj-ul-Qur'an Publications, 2011).
14. Edward Gibbon, *The History of the Decline and Fall of the Roman Empire*, ed. David Womersley (Penguin, 1994), vol. 3, p. 564.

15. Pope Francis, *The Joy of the Gospel* (Libreria Editrice Vaticana, 2013), par. 253.
16. Christopher Bail, *Terrified: How Anti-Muslim Fringe Organizations Became Mainstream* (Princeton University Press, 2015), pp. 114–21, on six centers for the dissemination of false information.
17. Pew Research Center, "The Future of the World Religions: Population Growth Projections, 2010–2050," Apr. 2, 2015.
18. Pope Francis, op. cit., par. 254: "As Christians, we can also benefit from these [Muslim] treasures built up over many centuries, which can help us better to live our own beliefs."
19. Jonathan A. C. Brown, *Misquoting Muhammad: The Challenge and Choices of Interpreting the Prophet's Legacy* (Oneworld, 2014), pp. 238–41, 302–5.
20. The Brennan Center for Justice has been keeping track of these legislative maneuvers ever since 2013: Andrew Cohen, "Foreign Law Bans Demonize Islamic Faith," Brennan Center for Justice, May 24, 2013.
21. Manya Brachear Pashman, "Wheaton College Could Face Long-Term Fallout over Professor Controversy," *Chicago Tribune*, Feb. 22, 2016.
22. Thomas Fuller, "The Right to Say 'God' Divides a Diverse Nation," *New York Times*, Nov. 3, 2014.
23. *The Study Quran: A New Translation and Commentary* (HarperOne, 2015).
24. M. A. S. Abdel Haleem, *The Qur'an: A New Translation*, reprinted with corrections (Oxford University Press, 2010).

Part I

Iraq: The Cost of Ignorance

CHAPTER 1

Secular Ignorance

The amazing thing about our Iraq war is not that we made such a colossal misjudgment, igniting the long-term series of explosions that have given us the Islamic State, but that we did it so blithely. It was supposed to spread peace and freedom throughout the region. It has instead spread death; it has uprooted populations; it has reanimated hatreds. It was presented as a generous favor we were doing the country, almost like picking up a person hit by a car. It was such an easy thing to do that it would be criminally idiotic not to do it. Supporters of the war vied with each other on this theme, each striving to make it seem easier than the other. No one in authority showed any awareness that there were religious grounds for the opposition of a Shia majority to Saddam's government using Sunni businessmen, Ba'ath Party members, and army officers to rule the country. It was all just a secular conflict between people yearning for American-style democracy and a despot. Since the people of Iraq wanted their freedom, and we were giving it to them, what could go wrong?

George W. Bush: "We're not going to have any casualties."[1]

George W. Bush: "It was unlikely that there would be internecine warfare between the different religious and ethnic groups."[2]

Dick Cheney: "We will, in fact, be greeted as liberators. . . . It will go relatively quickly . . . weeks rather than months. . . . The streets in Basra and Baghdad are sure to erupt in joy."[3]

Dick Cheney: "Once we start this, Saddam is toast."[4]

Donald Rumsfeld: "[Our military] can do the job and finish it fast . . . five days or five weeks or five months, but it certainly isn't going to last any longer than that. . . . It has nothing to do with the religion."[5]

Kenneth Adelman: "Liberating Iraq would be a cakewalk." . . . "Desert Storm II would be a walk in the park."[6]

Paul Wolfowitz: "They will greet us as liberators, and that will help us keep [troop] requirements down."[7]

Richard Perle: "Support for Saddam, including within his military organization, will collapse at the first whiff of gunpowder. . . . Now it isn't going to be over in 24 hours, but it isn't going to be months either."[8]

George Tenet: "It's a slam dunk."[9]

Giddy self-congratulations were raining all over the landscape before ever a bomb was dropped on Iraq. To judge from such program notes, we might have been engaging in a musical-comedy war, or joining the Marx Brothers in happy combat over Freedonia.

At first, the cheerful war seemed a hit, fulfilling the rhetorical investment of its producers. Within three weeks, Baghdad fell and Saddam's statue was photogenically pulled down. By the sixth week, President Bush suited up in battle jacket, navy helmet, and ejection harness, then climbed into "Navy One," an S-3B Viking warplane, and—after a few minutes' (thirty-mile) flight—was landed on the aircraft carrier USS *Abraham Lincoln,* which was decorated with a huge banner, made by the White House, declaring "Mission Accomplished." After walking photogenically around the deck in his flight gear for half an hour, the president changed into a civilian suit and delivered a speech declaring, "Major combat operations in Iraq have ended. In the battle of Iraq, the United States and our allies have prevailed."

Chris Matthews said of Bush on TV: "He won the war." The navy warplane, after taking the president back to land, was put on permanent display in the National Naval Aviation Museum in Pensacola, Florida. Busts of Bush in his flight jacket were offered for sale online. So were action figure toys of him in the full gear he wore on the carrier deck. The war had seemed miraculously easy. Democracy had come to the Middle East. Though it is usually tendentious to invoke Fascism, there is one resemblance here to Mussolini's theatrical approach to war. As Denis Mack Smith wrote:

> Mussolini also by instinct saw the usefulness of creating the impression that he could win easily and without great disturbance to the ordinary life of the nation. . . . Fascism continued to think it a matter for boasting that so little was demanded from Italy and that there was no general mobilization. To put this differently, resources were considered to be less usefully spent in war production than in fueling the great propaganda industry that was trying to convince ordinary citizens that all was well.[10]

Even as the Iraq cakewalk was turning into a death trap, a chipper tone was maintained by Secretary of Defense Rumsfeld, who dismissed the riot of looting with the words, "Stuff happens."[11] Sunni insurgents were only "pockets of dead-enders," he maintained.[12] And "freedom's untidy."[13] This just proved that freedom had come to Freedonia. Douglas Feith, Rumsfeld's undersecretary who had predicted that Iraqis would throw flowers on the arriving U.S. troops, was asked why this did not happen. He said the citizens were still afraid of Saddam, even after he was overthrown, but "they had flowers in their minds."[14]

To materialize these flowers in the Iraqis' minds was a task given to President Bush's personal proconsul for Iraq, Paul Bremer. He decided that all the remnants of Saddam's dictatorship should be erased. He began with the Ba'ath Party, whose largely Sunni membership included many business leaders, administrators, and security officers. Bremer's predecessor, Jay Garner, alerted him to what a CIA expert had warned:

> "If you put this [order] out, you're going to drive between 30,000 and 50,000 Ba'athists underground before nightfall. You will put 50,000 people on the street, underground and mad at Americans." And those 50,000 were the most powerful, well-connected elites from all walks of life.[15]

Ousting the Ba'ath Party was bad enough; but a week later Bremer disbanded the Iraqi army, planning to create a new one out of thin air.

> Overnight some 385,000 soldiers, plus another 285,000 employees of the Ministry of Interior—the home of police and domestic security services—were without jobs. Abruptly terminating the livelihood of these men created a vast pool of humiliated, antagonized, politicized men, many of whom were armed. It also represented a major setback in restoring order. As Colonel

John Agoglia, the deputy chief of planning at Central Command, said, "That was the day we snatched defeat from the jaws of victory."[16]

Bremer had given the motive and the means for an insurgency that has never ended. The chain of disasters initiated then has been facilely explained in retrospect, and the explanations are as misconceived as was the rationale for the war. We are still being told that we went to war only because "the intelligence was bad." The CIA gets blamed for telling President Bush that (a) Saddam Hussein was behind the 9/11 attack; and (b) Saddam had or was rapidly getting weapons of mass destruction; and (c) because of 9/11 and because of WMD we had to remove him instantly by "regime change." Much subsequent debate about the Iraq war has been concentrated on repeating or refuting these three assertions.

But all three miss the real point. There was a clearly announced plan for removing Saddam even before the 9/11 attacks, even before George W. Bush was elected president, and the plan was actually carried out by some of those who first proposed it. In January 1998, when Bill Clinton was still president, he received an open letter from the Project for the New American Century, signed by past and future members of Republican administrations, along with some academics and activists, numbering eighteen in all. The letter, published three and a half years before the 9/11 attacks, called for "the removal of Saddam Hussein's regime from power," a removal by force, since "diplomacy is clearly failing." It urged this course "to protect our vital interests in the Gulf" and for the safety "of our friends and allies like Israel and the moderate Arab states." President Clinton was told that he must act on his own to avoid being "crippled by a misguided insistence on unanimity in the UN Security Council."[17]

What was this Project for the New American Century? It was a group founded a year earlier by William Kristol and Robert Kagan, whose program had been published in *Foreign Affairs* (July/ August 1996) as "Toward a Neo-Reaganite Foreign Policy." The Project's "Statement of Principles" was signed in 1997 by twenty-five men and women, including future vice president Dick Cheney and future secretary of defense Donald Rumsfeld.[18] The group had a regular outlet for its views, since Kristol had launched in 1995 a journal, the *Weekly Standard*, founded with the help of $3 million every year from Australian-born publishing baron Rupert Murdoch. Their practical goal was stated in a *Weekly Standard* editorial titled "Saddam Must Go." This was published on November 17, 1997, almost four years before the attacks of September 11, 2001.

A mere week after those attacks, the Project authors wrote another open letter to a president, this time to George Bush, repeating what had been urged on President Clinton. It was signed by forty-one people, those who had signed the first letter (minus some who had already entered the Bush administration) plus new recruits to the cause. It is no wonder that when the attacks occurred, veterans of the Project like Cheney and Rumsfeld recognized at once that this was their chance to do what they had long been advocating—take out Saddam. Rumsfeld remembered that his deputy, Paul Wolfowitz, brought this up with President Bush at Camp David immediately after 9/11, where he said, "Iraq must have been helping them" (those who attacked the World Trade Center).[19]

Wolfowitz was just acting on his earlier plea that the U.S. should strike Iraq as soon as "we find the right way to do it."[20] The right way was found on 9/11. In two sentences, the Project's new letter brushed past the al-Qaeda forces that brought down the towers, to concentrate again (in six sentences) on the main target, Saddam Hussein (who had nothing to do with the attack):

It may be that the Iraqi government provided assistance in some form to the recent attack on the United States. But even if evidence does not link Iraq directly to the attack, any strategy aiming at the eradication of terrorism and its sponsors must include a determined effort to remove Saddam Hussein from power in Iraq. Failure to undertake such an effort will constitute an early and perhaps decisive surrender in the war on international terrorism.[21]

Thomas Friedman of the *New York Times,* who had himself supported the war but on different grounds, was not exaggerating when he said the immediate concentration on Iraq came from the Project for the New American Century, whose members were now called the neoconservatives:

It's the war the neoconservatives marketed. Those people had an idea to sell when September 11 came, and they sold it. Oh boy, did they sell it. So this is not a war that the masses demanded. This is a war of an elite. I could give you the names of 25 people (all of whom are at the moment within a five-block radius of this [New York] office) who, if you had exiled them to a desert island a year and a half ago, the Iraq war would not have happened.[22]

Why did the Project focus so early and ardently on Saddam? He was just one element in that "policy for a new century" that Kristol and Kagan had outlined in *Foreign Affairs* and incorporated in the Project's Statement of Principles. That Project grew from a grand vision of the world after Ronald Reagan's defeat of Communism. The fall of the Berlin Wall created a unipolar world, where only one superpower remained. After such an enormous struggle, one might expect, there should be a stepping down of massive military expenditures. The Project said this would be a shirking of duty. According to those planning "the new American century," America should arm and spend to get all the benefits of a "benevolent global hegemony." Though George W. Bush had campaigned against "nation building," and said his administration would have a "humble" foreign policy, 9/11 made him adopt the unipolar vision of the neoconservatives, for which they applauded him.

Speaking at West Point on June 1, 2002, the president said, "The United States possesses unprecedented—and unequaled—strength and influence in the world. . . . This position comes with unparalleled responsibilities, obligations, and opportunity." The State Department followed Bush's lead, issuing a new strategy in September of 2002, to "use this moment of opportunity to extend the benefits of freedom across the globe." This was a momentous shift in policy, framed precisely to justify the invasion of Iraq. The earlier policy had been one of containment and deterrence. The new one was for regime change and preemption.[23] Since international Communism no longer constricted us, we could bring democracies into being and strengthen them, toppling tyrants with our unmatched power. We must not, according to the *Weekly Standard*, be "unwilling to shoulder the responsibilities of global leadership."[24]

One of the easy (but neglected) topplings had been that of Saddam in 1990, when the first President Bush threw him out of Kuwait. The Kristol folk condemned Bush I's failure to finish that easy task, and meant to complete it as an old order of business before going on to the new democracies America would set up. A typical publication in the *Weekly Standard* at this time (October 15, 2001) was Max Boot's "The Case for American Empire," which detailed all the good things to be accomplished by "a liberal and humanitarian imperialism." Doing them was admittedly "a long-term task" that would mean not only maintaining but increasing American power. Once we had toppled Saddam, we would need the resources to reap all the benefits from turning Iraq into "a beacon of hope for the oppressed peoples of the Middle East."

> With American seriousness and credibility thus restored, we will enjoy fruitful cooperation from the region's many opportunists, who will show a newfound eagerness to be helpful in our larger task of rolling up the international terror network that threatens us. Over the years, America has earned opprobrium in the Arab word for its realpolitik backing of repressive dictators like Hosni Mubarak and the Saudi royal family. This could be the chance to right the scales, to establish the first Arab democracy, and to show the Arab people that America is as committed to freedom for them as we were for the people of East Europe.

The Bush administration was so eager to seize the opportunity to topple Saddam that it could not wait for Commissioner Hans Blix to finish the International Atomic Energy Agency's search for weapons of mass destruction on the ground in Iraq—instead, Wolfowitz had the CIA investigate *Blix*.[25] Bush assembled a "Coalition of the Willing," states willing to join the war on Iraq—a coalition that was made up largely of small states that were given increased American foreign aid in return for using their names.[26] The only important member of the "coalition" was the United Kingdom, and Prime Minister Tony Blair's engineering of that move has deeply blackened his historical record.[27] The French were vilified in Congress for not joining the coalition—a committee had congressional cafeterias change their menu item "French Fries" to "Freedom Fries"—a sneer that remained on the menus for three years.[28]

Underlying the secularists' plunge into war was a sweeping vision enunciated by a charter member of the Project for the New American Century—Francis Fukuyama. He had been a signer of both letters to the presidents and a classmate with Kristol as they got their doctorates in political science from Harvard. ("Frank" was two years behind "Bill," so he was able to move into his former apartment in Cambridge.)[29] Though he had participated in the normal cult of neoconservatism's gurus (Leo Strauss, Allan Bloom, Harvey Mansfield), Fukuyama offered the promise of new depth by his study of Hegel (as filtered through the work of Alexandre Kojève), asking the question: What happens to a teleological philosophy of history when the telos is reached? If a dog catches the car he is chasing, what does he do with it? As Hegelians in Europe had asked, What would be left for the last man to do?

Fukuyama offered an answer to this question in an article for the *National Interest* called "The End of History?" The thesis of the article was arresting:

> The triumph of the West, of the Western *idea,* is evident first of all in the total exhaustion of viable systematic alternatives to Western liberalism. . . . What we may be witnessing is not just the end of the Cold War, or the passing of a particular period of post-war history, but the end of history as such: that is, the end point of mankind's ideological evolution and the universalization of Western liberal democracy as the final form of human government.[30]

The article, which appeared in the summer 1989 issue of the journal, was already being widely discussed when, in November of the same year, the Berlin Wall came down, seeming to validate Fukuyama's claim that American Liberal Democracy had given all rival ideologies a permanent knockout blow.

The popularity of Fukuyama's idea led the Free Press to offer him a $600,000 advance for a book based on the article. He took the occasion to quit his government job, working in George H. W. Bush's State Department, to devote his time to lecturing and writing.[31] The book, developed from his *National Interest* article, was *The End of History and the Last Man*, and its publication in 1992 dwarfed the intense attention given the article. It developed a secular eschatology, the counterpart (intended as a replacement) of all the religious views of the End Time. The original eschatologies led to some kind of final battle and judgment for a heaven that would replace life on earth. Unlike those, Fukuyama's End Time was just a permanent extension of life on earth, fulfilling Kant's dream of a permanent peace. His final battle had already occurred, and the heaven it led to was the American form of Liberal Democracy.

The twentieth century had pitted the last three great ideological systems—Fascism, Communism, and Liberal Democracy—against each other for control of the world. The victory of Liberal Democracy over its two rivals had left no other plausible system for that task. The only remaining issue was how America would use this victory for the extension of its system over holdouts of local despotism—which were condemned to be local and controllable because they had no appealing ideology aspiring to universality, as the Big Three had done. Fukuyama gave Islam as the perfect example of such a local force that would be self-limiting, up against the only remaining universal system. As he wrote in the *National Interest* article:

> In the contemporary world only Islam has offered a theocratic state as a political alternative to both liberalism and communism. But the doctrine has little appeal for non-Muslims, and it is hard to believe that the movement will take on any universal significance. Other less organized religious impulses

have been successfully satisfied within the sphere of personal life that is permitted in liberal societies.

In the book, he was even more dismissive of Islam:

> The days of Islam's cultural conquests, it would seem, are over: it can win back lapsed adherents, but has no resonance for young people in Berlin, Tokyo, or Moscow. And while nearly a billion people are culturally Islamic—one-fifth of the world's population—they cannot challenge liberal democracy on its own territory on the level of ideas.[32]

Liberalism overcomes every challenge. It blocks threats by satisfying needs, which religion had failed to do. As he wrote in the *National Interest* article:

> Modern liberalism itself was historically a consequence of the weakness of religiously-based societies which, failing to agree on the nature of the good life, could not provide even the minimal preconditions of peace and stability.[33]

Get rid of religion, and you finally escape religious wars. In the book, we read:

> The fundamentally un-warlike character of liberal societies is evident in the extraordinarily peaceful relations they maintain among one another. There is now a substantial body of literature noting the fact that there have been few, if any, instances of one liberal democracy going to war with another.[34]

Some objected that, with nothing to fight about, people might have nothing to care about. His end of history sounded less interesting than the world as it was when we still had history. It ended not with a bang but a whimper. He admitted this was a problem, wondering how the last man would be able to engage in "thymotic" activity—from the Greek *thymos*, "spiritedness," which one of his teachers, Harvey Mansfield, had long glorified as the essence of "manliness."[35] Fukuyama said that we must learn to be content with what William James had called the moral equivalent of war. One outlet for such striving would be the daring of the right wing's manly entrepreneur.

> The first and most important of these outlets in a liberal society is entrepreneurship and other forms of economic activity. . . . It is in the very design of democratic capitalist countries like the United States that the most talented and ambitious natures should tend to go into business, rather than into politics, the military, universities, or the church.[36]

But he wondered if peaceful competition would satisfy people of "great thymos":

> How long megalothymia will be satisfied with metaphorical wars and symbolic victories is an open question. One suspects that some people will not be satisfied until they prove themselves by that very act that constituted their humanness at the beginning of history: they will want to risk their lives in a violent battle.[37]

Luckily, his last men will not have to go cold turkey on their warring manliness. Even in the time of its "benevolent hegemony," the United States will have the power (and the duty) to clean up pockets of despotism or prod reluctant societies into the democracy that brings them ultimate peace. To reverse the saying of Dante,

"In His will is our peace," he offers, "In our will is your peace": *in NOSTRA voluntad e VESTRA pace*. Fukuyama's book describes a therapeutic substitute for the real wars that occurred before the end of history:

> A liberal democracy that could fight a short and decisive war every generation or so to defend its own liberty and independence would be far healthier and more satisfied than one that experienced nothing but continuous peace.[38]

That is a perfect prediction of what the Bush government thought it was doing with the Iraq war. A little "shock and awe" would prod others to see that resistance to American-style democracy had lost its point. Tyrants were just trying to get messy old history started again, after the "scholars" had declared that it was over. This is the kind of healthy war the *Weekly Standard* was urging on President Bush just before he invaded Iraq:

> A devastating knockout blow against Saddam Hussein, followed by an American-sponsored effort to rebuild Iraq and put it on a path toward democratic governance, would have a seismic impact on the Arab world—for the better.[39]

Michael Ledeen, a consultant to the Pentagon, gave a franker paraphrase of Fukuyama's doctrine on homeopathic war (the lesser evil curing the greater). "Every ten years or so, the United States needs to pick up some small crappy little country and throw it against the wall, just to show the world we mean business."[40] Saving freedom is no work for the squeamish.

Soon, of course, the neoconservatives had to crawl out from under what they had written pre-Iraq. Most said that the war was a great idea spoiled by bad execution. But few if any of them said that they had been blinded by secularism to the cultural (largely religious) complexities of the Middle East. They had been warned of this by a man who had taught or conferred with them in the past, Samuel Huntington of Harvard. Huntington rejected the end-of-history thesis in his 1996 book, *The Clash of Civilizations.*[41] Like Fukuyama, he had first aired his argument in a scholarly journal. Like him, he stated it with a question mark: "The Clash of Civilizations?"[42] Three years later, he sharpened the attack in another article (with no question mark), "The West: Unique, Not Universal."[43] His widely anticipated book was about to appear, and one of the co-founders of the Project for the New American Century, Robert Kagan, rushed to the defense of Fukuyama. The Project had called for a "benign American hegemony." Huntington said it was neither benign nor final. "American hegemony is receding."[44] Universalism is just another name for imperialism, and is therefore immoral. "The time has come for the West to abandon the illusion of universalism. . . . What is universalism to the West is imperialism to the rest."[45]

Kagan counterattacked in the *Weekly Standard* (where else?) with an article called "Harvard Hates America." Huntington, in denying American hegemony, set up nine separate cultural hegemonies. That meant he was denying "American exceptionalism," a core belief of the neoconservatives.[46] He was embracing a relativistic "multiculturalism," a favorite enemy of the neoconservatives. Kagan convicted Huntington of heretically denying that "human liberty is a universal value and is spreading."[47] This is the premise that the Bush administration would act upon in Iraq—the belief that all Iraqis yearned for freedom and would be pleased to see Saddam go. Huntington had thus joined "the rest" in their opposition to "the West." As an anti-American he was living proof that "Harvard hates America."

When it turned out that Iraqis were greeting U.S. troops with

IEDs instead of flowers, the neoconservatives had to invent ways to avoid eating their own words. When rejoicing over the "mission accomplished" faded, neoconservatives spent the next seven years of George W. Bush's time in office tiptoeing away from the president. He should not have let the looting and insurgency go on as long as they did. General Petraeus should have been put in charge earlier, to rectify a foundering effort. At last some of the neoconservatives directed at Bush II what they had long condemned in Bush I—he did not know how to finish the job. However, when President Obama took office in 2004, they could make him the scapegoat for Bush's failures. Kristol finally made that the regnant neoconservative position. As he wrote in a *Washington Post* op-ed: "When President Obama took office, Iraq was calm, al-Qaeda was weakened and ISIS did not exist. . . . The Obama administration threw it all away."[48]

But Fukuyama, who was farther out on the limb than any of his fellow neoconservatives, went much farther than they did in dissociating himself from his fellows. He did not simply saw off the limb. He chopped down the tree. He said he was not all that close to the neoconservatives, they were not important anyway, they did not influence the Iraq war, and he never supported the war (though he signed both letters urging two presidents to overthrow Saddam). He was taking a new way to end history—by rewriting it. In his 2006 book, *America at the Crossroads,* he said that he, like Marx, had been thinking of long-term inevitabilities, while the Bush people, like Lenin, rushed toward an immediate showdown.[49] They had a shallow view of "regime change"—as just knocking off Saddam—while he took the deeper, the true, the "Straussian" meaning of "regime," which includes culture and religion.[50] So he was not that far from Huntington after all.

The year after he published this muted palinode, Fukuyama

came clean on what he was doing in *America at the Crossroads*. He told an audience in San Francisco that he wrote the book as a way of "bailing out of the neocon way of looking at the world." Not that he had ever held that "neocon way" absolutely. In fact, he now claimed that the neoconservative movement was nothing but "Bill Kristol and a fax machine." Kristol would fax his letters around and some would sign them. "I signed his letters a couple of times," but this had no effect in the real world. It was just one man's quirks, which Fukuyama barely adverted to. (He had written his book in a fit of absentmindedness.) Nor had he ever believed in a benign American hegemony. He thought the West would prevail as a set of "multiple and overlapping democratic entities"—like Kojève's belief that the European Union marked the end of history. When the moderator of the San Francisco program, Stewart Brand, noticed that the European Union was not faring so well in 2007 (when the immigrant problem was just beginning), Fukuyama had to admit that this *was* a problem. But Fukuyama had accomplished his own new mission—to put an end to his own personal history.

Unfortunately, the Iraq war could not be erased so easily. George Bush had accomplished his own historical mission, though he did not know, yet, what it was. His real mission was to create the Islamic State, supplying terrorists with all the propaganda they could wish for.

When George W. Bush declared combat operations in Iraq to be over from the flight deck of the *Abraham Lincoln* on May 1, 2003, 172 Americans had been killed in action and another 552 wounded. By the end of 2003, American casualties totaled 580 dead and 2,420 wounded. When Bush left office in January 2009, 4,539 U.S. servicemen and women had lost their lives in Iraq. Another 30,740 had been wounded.

These tragic figures pale beside the number of Iraqi casualties. Saddam had been overthrown. But no weapons of mass destruction had been found, and the United States had sullied its image as the world's standard-bearer of democracy.[51]

NOTES

1. Alan Cooperman, "Bush Predicted No Iraq Casualties, Robertson Says," *Washington Post*, Oct. 21, 2004.
2. President George Bush to Tony Blair, Jan. 21, 2003, from David Manning notes of the meeting, quoted by Don Van Natta, Jr., in *New York Times*, Mar. 27, 2006.
3. Vice President Cheney, *Meet the Press*, Mar. 16, 2003. Press conference, Aug. 26, 2002, NBC News.
4. Cheney to Prince Bandar, Jan. 11, 2003. In Dick Cheney, *In My Time* (Threshold, 2011), p. 394.
5. Secretary of Defense Donald Rumsfeld, interview on Infinity Broadcasting Corporation, Nov. 14, 2002.
6. Pentagon Defense Policy Board member Adelman, op-ed in *Washington Post*, Feb. 13, 2002; headline of article in *Times* of London, Aug. 29, 2002.
7. Deputy Secretary of Defense Wolfowitz, testimony before the House Budget Committee, Feb. 27, 2003.
8. Chairman of the Pentagon Defense Policy Board Perle, on *Wide Angle* (PBS), July 11, 2002.
9. CIA director George Tenet to President Bush, Dec. 21, 2002, on the existence of weapons of mass destruction in Iraq. After denying for years that he had said that, Tenet at last confessed in public, "Those are the two dumbest words I ever said." Bob Woodward, *State of Denial: Bush at War; Part III* (Simon & Schuster, 2006), pp. 303–4.
10. Denis Mack Smith, *Mussolini's Roman Empire* (Viking, 1976), p. 239.
11. Department of Defense News Briefing, Apr. 11, 2003.
12. Associated Press report, June 18, 2003.
13. Department of Defense News Briefing, Apr. 11, 2003.
14. Jeffrey Goldberg, "A Little Learning: What Douglas Feith Knew, and When He Knew It," *New Yorker*, May 9, 2005.
15. Bob Woodward, *State of Denial*, p. 194.
16. Jean Edward Smith, *Bush* (Simon & Schuster, 2016), p. 373.

17. Project for the New American Century, Letter to the Honorable William J. Clinton, Jan. 26, 1998.

18. See Scott McConnell, "The *Weekly Standard*'s War," *American Conservative,* Nov. 21, 2005.

19. Donald Rumsfeld, interviewed by Sean Hannity on Fox News, Feb. 8, 2011, and see Richard A. Clarke, *Against All Enemies* (Free Press, 2004), p. 30.

20. Paul Wolfowitz, quoted with approval by Lawrence Kaplan and William Kristol, *The War over Iraq* (Encounter Books, 2003), p. 70.

21. Project for the New American Century, Letter to the Honorable George W. Bush, Sept. 20, 2001. This was signed by several who had signed the earlier letter to President Clinton, including Richard Perle and Francis Fukuyama.

22. Friedman interview, *Ha'aretz,* Apr. 3, 2003. Friedman goes on to admit that there was popular pressure to avenge the 9/11 atrocities, but this retaliatory impulse would not have been focused at once on Saddam and Iraq without the Project members both inside and outside the Bush administration.

23. The new strategy was expounded and praised in a book that was ready almost at the moment when the attack on Iraq began. See Kaplan and Kristol, cited in note 20.

24. Robert Kagan and William Kristol, "What to Do About Iraq," *Weekly Standard,* Jan. 21, 2002.

25. Walter Pincus and Colum Lynch, "Skirmish on Iraq Inspections," *Washington Post,* Apr. 15, 2002.

26. Laura McClure, "Coalition of the Billing—or Unwilling?," *Salon,* Mar. 12, 2003.

27. Desmond Tutu, "Why I Had No Choice but to Spurn Tony Blair," *Guardian,* Sept. 1, 2012.

28. Jamie Wilson, "French Fries Protester Regrets War Jibe," *Guardian,* May 24, 2005.

29. Francis Fukuyama, "*The End of History* Revisited," a lecture at the Long Now Foundation, San Francisco, June 28, 2007 (available on DVD from San Simeon Films).

30. Francis Fukuyama, "The End of History?," *National Interest,* Summer 1989.

31. Francis Fukuyama, interviewed when the Fukuyama phenomenon was in its early blossoming: Nicholas Wroe, "History's Pallbearer," *Guardian,* May 10, 2002.

32. Francis Fukuyama, *The End of History and the Last Man* (Free Press, 1992), p. 46.

33. Fukuyama, "The End of History?" In his *Guardian* interview (note 31 above) Fukuyama showed that he has never been interested in his ancestral religion

from Japan nor in the Congregationalism of his father ("That kind of Protestantism is barely religion"). He calls himself an agnostic, and says, "I've found it quite a struggle to think of myself as a believer" (the Long Now lecture; see note 29 above). No one is required to show interest in religion for him- or herself; but to have none for the religion of other peoples should be a disqualification for the social sciences. Fukuyama, who is cosmopolitan in some ways, is oddly provincial in others. According to the interview with the admiring Nicholas Wroe, Fukuyama learned four foreign languages—but not the Japanese spoken by his parents and grandparents.

34. Fukuyama, *The End of History and the Last Man*, pp. 262–63.

35. Harvey C. Mansfield, *Manliness* (Yale University Press, 2006).

36. Fukuyama, *The End of History*, pp. 315–16.

37. Ibid., p. 329.

38. Ibid.

39. Kagan and Kristol, op. cit.

40. Michael Ledeen, quoted approvingly in Jonah Goldberg, "Baghdad Delenda Est, Part Two," *National Review*, Apr. 23, 2002. Ledeen had earlier, three months after the 9/11 attacks, said that hegemonic America must use the anger caused by those attacks to remodel the whole Middle East:

> We will not rest until we have avenged our dead, we will not be sated until we have had the blood of every miserable little tyrant in the Middle East, until every leader of every cell of the terror network is dead or locked securely away, and every last drooling anti-Semitic and anti-American mullah, imam, sheikh, and ayatollah is either singing the praises of the United States or pumping gasoline, for a dime a gallon, in an American military base near the Arctic Circle. If we send in the United Nations, and turn over the construction of civil society to the NGOs, we're losers. (Michael Ledeen, "We Must Be Imperious, Ruthless, and Relentless," *Jewish World Review*, Dec. 11, 2001.)

41. Samuel P. Huntington, *The Clash of Civilizations and the Remaking of World Order* (Simon & Schuster, 1996), p. 31.

42. Samuel Huntington, "The Clash of Civilizations?," *Foreign Affairs*, Summer 1993.

43. Samuel Huntington, "The West: Unique, Not Universal," *Foreign Affairs*, Nov./Dec. 1996.

44. Ibid., p. 40.

45. Ibid., p. 41.

46. Kaplan and Kristol (op. cit., p. 64), pronounced the dogma:

> American exceptionalism—a belief in the uniqueness and the virtue of the American political system that, when translated into foreign policy terms, offers the United States as a model for the world. It is a model because faith in the universal ideal of freedom, not a blood-and-soil nationalism, is what defines the America idea.

47. Robert Kagan, "Harvard Hates America," *Weekly Standard*, Dec. 8, 1996.
48. William Kristol, "We Were Right to Fight in Iraq," *Washington Post*, May 20, 2015.
49. Francis Fukuyama, *America at the Crossroads: Democracy, Power, and the Neo-conservative Legacy* (Yale University Press, 2006), pp. 54–55.
50. Ibid., pp. 29–30.
51. Jean Edward Smith, op. cit., pp. 379–80.

CHAPTER 2

Religious Ignorance

Tantum religio potuit suadere malorum.

So suasive is religion to our bane.

—LUCRETIUS[1]

Secularism was hailed as a triumphant movement in the second half of the twentieth century. It seemed so sweeping that a project of the American Academy of Arts and Sciences predicted in 1967 that it would be regnant by the year 2000. Its "Year 2000" program commissioned ambitious studies claiming that social predictions were more sure than scientific ones, more "surprise free," since social attitudes are more firmly rooted in human habit.[2] Yet a mere eleven years after the Academy of Arts and Sciences launched this triumphalist secular study, it commissioned an even more expensive and ambitious program based on an exactly opposite premise—that religious fundamentalism was burgeoning all over the world, a comeback for religiosity that could not be denied, however puzzling it seemed, and one that anticipated the zealous terrorism of the twenty-first century's opening years.

The year 2000 now assumed a different complexion. People were beginning to remember old myths about a new millennium as an end-of-the-world time. A panic was stirred up over new dates undoing all the numbers in our interacting digital instruments. This became known as the Y2K problem, or the millennium crash (YTK Bug). It would be the classical revenge for technological hubris. As if to reactivate every kind of superstition, 2000 was also a leap year, with whatever curse that was supposed to bring. Few now remembered that the year 2000 had been projected, in studies from the 1960s, as the target date for secularism's triumph.[3]

Under this froth of a passing hysteria there was a real and certifiable "revival of revivalism" that had been going on for decades. This was the reason for the Fundamentalism Project of the academy, supported with extra funds from the MacArthur Foundation. There were new energies of militant and/or mystical sects around the world. Tremors of it were first discerned in America in 1976, when Jimmy Carter was elected president as a "born-again" Christian. But the real political impact of evangelicals was not felt till the next election (1980), when the Moral Majority, founded in 1979 by Jerry Falwell, opposed Carter and supported Ronald Reagan. Jimmy Carter was not evangelical *enough* on issues, since he did not express opposition to evolution, feminism, abortion, environmentalism, and fetal-tissue use, while Reagan was sound on all these matters. He even toyed with "the prophecies" of the End Time, and Israel's role in it. The Moral Majority as an organization has faded, but the religious right is still fighting on all these fronts and more.

The Fundamentalism Project, chaired by Martin Marty and Scott Appleby, gathered the studies of two hundred international scholars working over a period of eight years, charting how people were going back to literal interpretations of their sacred writings—the Torah, the Talmud, the Halakha, the Qur'an, the Bible, the (Sikh) Granth Sahib—as "true and accurate in all particulars."[4] How could a dying religious attitude, scheduled for elimination by the end of the twentieth century—already, as it were, being measured for its coffin—dance away from the dirge with renewed vitality? More pointedly, how could this escape from the cemetery occur simultaneously all over the world, just when secularism, science, and progress seemed to be surging toward victory? Someone had not been guarding the tomb. The ghost had got out.

The project found that this religious revival was not something separable from the secular trends described by the Year 2000 project. The former, in fact, grew from the latter. Fundamentalism was happening when it did, at the rate it did, precisely in the places and at the rate where secularism was occurring: "The defining and distinctive structural cause of fundamentalist movement is secularization."[5] This was the conclusion reached by many other social scientists. Samuel Huntington wrote in 1996:

> It is too much to expect that a large number of different causes would have produced simultaneous and similar developments in most parts of the world. A global phenomenon demands a global explanation. . . . The most obvious, most salient, and most powerful cause of the global religious resurgence is precisely what was supposed to cause the death of religion: the processes of social, economic, and cultural modernization that swept across the world in the second half of the twentieth century.[6]

The cultural anthropologist Olivier Roy reached the same conclusion as the Fundamentalism Project. In his book *Holy Ignorance* (2013), he wrote:

There is a close link between secularization and religious revivalism, which is not a reaction against secularization but the product of it. Secularism engenders religion. . . . We are witnessing a shift of the traditional forms of religious practice— Catholicism, Hanafi Islam, classic Protestant denominations such as Anglicanism and Methodism—toward more fundamentalist and charismatic forms of religiosity (evangelicalism, Pentecostalism, Salafism, Tablighi Jamaat, neo-Sufism, Lubavich).[7]

In America, examples of holy ignorance were on display, early in the twenty-first century, as Republican politicians catered to the growing number of politically active evangelicals in America. Asked whether they agreed to the truth of evolution or climate change, a common response was "I am not a scientist." That statement, if made by many people, would be a humble admission of scientific incompetence, expressing a willingness to listen to and learn from people who *are* scientists. But coming from people with a *holy* ignorance, it means "I am obliged not to know, where the godless force of science must be resisted if we are to remain spiritually alive." Not-knowing becomes a duty. What matters is not the evidence on any individual matter, but the whole ethos and method of "godless" science.

Roy notes that this freedom from evidence allows evangelicals to float off even from the evidence in or about their own sacred texts. About the Bible he writes:

Evangelical Protestants follow it "to the letter," but a letter freed not only from the original language, but from language itself, in order to see no more than a simple message. . . . It does not question the veracity of the letter of the scriptures, but nor is it interested in the actual language of the text, nor, incidentally, in any specific language.[8]

Roy, from his French base, was not very interested in American evangelicals or he would have noted the way some American theologians justified their defiance of evidence. A theologian from Calvin College, Cornelius Van Til, argued that one's attitude toward evidence determines what one will take from it. He said that all forms of proof work from premises that are unproved—from what he called presuppositions, or (to use his fancier word) one's *Weltanschauung*.[9] They do not scrutinize the evidence of science or scripture but whether a scrutinizer brings to the matter a godless or a godly *Weltanschauung*. They say that scientists' initial error is to deny that they have any presuppositions. Such people fool themselves that they can be completely neutral and objective.

A cognate reaction against secular values can be seen in the anti-colonialism that remade the globe after World War II. European powers that had used the resources and logistics of their colonial dependencies during the war found that this had equipped the colonies for rebellion after the war. The leaders of rebellion used tools they had acquired from the colonizers. They wanted not only to free but to modernize their subject nations. This meant that they came to their own people from outside the indigenous culture they were "liberating." As Michael Walzer puts it:

> The liberationists have often gone to school with the oppressors, who commonly claim to represent a more "advanced" culture—materially, intellectually, and militarily.[10]

Walzer analyzes three cases of decolonization—Algeria throwing off French rule, Israel and India throwing off British rule. Spokesmen for the new regimes—men like Herzl, Weizmann, and Jabotinsky for Israel, Fanon and Ben Bella for Algeria, Nehru for India—tried to raise up native people as well as push away foreign rule. They wanted to imitate advances already made in the

European countries, in matters like democratic procedure, religious pluralism, or the emancipation of women. But in doing this, they created resistance in the temples or synagogues or mosques that had created the ethos they were challenging. Walzer notes:

> Even the leaders of these movements, when they exercised political power, did so with a sure sense that they knew what was best for their backward and often recalcitrant peoples. Then the backwardness came back—and the democracy that the liberationists created (even in Algeria, briefly, from 1989 to 1991) was the chief instrument of its return. "The present crisis of liberal democracy [in India]," writes the political theorist Rajeev Bhargava, "is due in large part to its own success."[11]

Leaders of this sort were simultaneously breaking political ties to an outside power and undermining the culture of the newly declared sovereign entities. As Murray Kempton wryly noted in 1966: "The way one African could communicate his hatred of French oppression to another African was only by speaking French."[12] So the story Michael Walzer tells is the same one Olivier Roy and Martin Marty outlined, that secularism set the stage for energetic opposition by fundamentalists: "The FLN [in Algeria] was a revolution in the making; resurgent Islam is the counterrevolution."[13] Everywhere the success of secularization undermined itself. Religion was supposed to die, but it refused to.

This is the massive worldwide phenomenon the neoconservatives were ignoring when they launched the invasion of Iraq. And when they ignored the relevant religiosities of the Middle East, they gave interpretive space to the fundamentalist religiosities in America. Donald Rumsfeld said that the invasion of Iraq had nothing to do with religion. The inadequacy of his understanding was matched by the people who said that conflict there had nothing to with anything

but religion. Senator Lindsey Graham spoke for many when, pre-
paring to run for president in 2015, he said:

> The longer it takes to destroy them, the more likely we are to
> get hit. . . . We are in a religious war. . . . Their way of life is
> motivated by religious teachings that require me and you to
> be killed, or enslaved, or converted. . . . They [our Muslim
> foes] cannot be accommodated. They cannot be negotiated
> with. They have to be eventually destroyed.[14]

Senator Graham was not an outlier or exception in the run-up
to the presidential election of 2016. The crowded field of Republican
candidates sounded, at times, as if they were running against Islam,
not against Democrats. Governor Scott Walker of Wisconsin, an
early favorite in the polls and in fund-raising, said that terrorists
were at "war against even the *handful* of reasonable, moderate followers of Islam" as if the *majority* of Muslims were behind every
terrorist attack around the world.[15] After President Obama confessed past Christian acts of violence at a National Prayer Break-
fast, recurring candidate Mike Huckabee, a Baptist minister and
former president of the Arkansas Baptist State Convention, said on
Fox News:

> Everything he [Obama] does is against what Christians stand
> for, and he's against the Jews in Israel. The one group of peo-
> ple that can know they have his undying, unfailing support
> would be the Muslim community. It doesn't matter whether
> it's the radical Muslim community or the more moderate Mus-
> lim community.[16]

Everything Obama did was against Christianity and for Islam? Not
only did Huckabee think there was a holy war on, but that

America's own president had enlisted on the other side, not that of all Christians and Jews. And Obama was said to war against his own American people with an "undying, unfailing" determination.

Another Republican candidate, Dr. Ben Carson, was running high in national polls when he said that he would oppose having Muslims run for president of the United States:

> If they are not willing to reject sharia and all the portions of it that are talked about in the Qur'an, if they are not willing to reject that, and subject that to American values and the Constitution, then of course I would [oppose them].[17]

Actually, there are no "portions" of the Qur'an that discuss Shari'ah. Though claiming to be a very religious man, Dr. Carson was not exempt from the religious ignorance that overcame politicians in 2016.

And this very religious man later endorsed the most spectacularly ignorant Republican candidate of 2016, Donald Trump, who wanted to create a religious test for entry into the United States, excluding all Muslims. What was his reason for this? He told Anderson Cooper on CNN that it was because "Islam hates us. . . . We can't allow people coming into this country who have this hatred of the United States." Asked in a subsequent debate whether he had reconsidered this sweeping judgment on a whole body of believers, he doubled down: "There's tremendous hatred, and I will stick with exactly what I said to Anderson Cooper."[18]

These are only the most visible people trying to incite a holy war. They try to prevent knowledge of the full range of attitudes and factions in the Muslim world. In such a climate, our know-nothings cry out against foreign know-nothings, who reciprocate the anger. We have had in America a growing chorus of people who say that Shari'ah is the enemy. The Qur'an is the enemy. Islam is the enemy. The less one knows about any of these things, they say, the better off is the country. This kind of religious fervor is regularly matched with a high degree of religious illiteracy. It becomes a patriotic duty to prevent the young from reading, or even reading about, the Qur'an.

It is a common practice of universities now to assign an important book (sometimes a controversial book) to incoming freshmen and have them write down their reaction to it. Then, during orientation week, the freshmen are split into discussion groups to air their opinions with each other and a professor (and sometimes with the author of the assigned reading, who has been invited to orientation). Incoming students are thus given a shared reading experience as a way of both breaking the ice with each other and introducing them to the critical method of university discourse. Often, the parents are interested in what their child will be doing at university, and they read the book or discuss it with the person going off to college, which encourages them to be a part of the student's college experience.[19]

In 2002, the University of North Carolina assigned for freshman reading a book called *Approaching the Qur'án,* by Michael Sells. The author is not a Muslim, nor a proselytizer for Islam. He tries to make an important but difficult book interesting by stressing its aesthetic quality, especially in its chanted form (the sessions were to hear recordings of its recitation). When a conservative organization called the Family Policy Network (FPN) heard of this, it sued in district court to prevent this as a violation of religious freedom. The FPN brought forward three teenage plaintiffs—one Roman Catholic, one evangelical, one Jewish—whose religious freedom would be denied by being "forced" to read a book outside their own tradition.

Actually, no one was being forced to read it. Alerted to possible objections, the university sent out a form that read: "If any students or their families are opposed to reading parts of the Qur'an because to do so is offensive to their own faith, they may choose not to read the book." Such students could opt to discuss only their reasons for doing so.[20] The suit was rejected in both the district and the appeals courts, the judge in the former case ruling that the book did not advocate Islam. But even when the courts had twice rejected the FPN argument against this exercise, the North Carolina House of Representatives voted to deny any state funds used in the exercise, a move that—had it been passed by the other branch of the legislature—would have endangered religious study programs in the sixteen schools of the state's university system.[21] The same dynamic that was shown in this lawmaking body has led states to rule against the supposed danger of observing Shari'ah law in state courts, schools, and legislative bodies.

Despite defeat of the FPN in the courts and in the legislature, right-wing clarions sounded against the dangers of reading about the Qur'an. Bill O'Reilly, Franklin (son of Billy) Graham, and William F. Buckley, Jr., denounced the university's action. Buckley wrote a column that said:

> The bowdlerizers at the University of North Carolina have got out a special edition of the Koran . . . designed to communicate the teachings of the Prophet. This edition is exorcised of any sentiments such as might have impelled the knights of 9/11 to plunge themselves and their steeds into live Americans, innocent of any infidelity to Islam, this side of not adhering to it.[22]

The Sells book is not a "special edition" of the Qur'an. It was not "got out" by the university. Nor bowdlerized by it. Nor "exorcised." Nor "designed to communicate the teachings of the Prophet" (as the two courts ruled). There is no evidence Mr. Buckley had read either the Qur'an or the Sells book. Nor that the Reverend Franklin Graham had done so—Graham was the man Mr. Buckley wrote his column to defend. Their concern was clearly to keep others as ignorant of the book as they had managed to remain. They assumed (on no evidence) that the book could have no meaning other than defense of mass murder.

This deliberate ignorance among the supporters of their own self-declared war on Islam had its proud equivalent in the government itself. Though he seemed to be just following the schedule drawn up for him by the Project for the New American Century, Bush constantly asserted that he was "the Decider," an impression Harry Truman also cultivated (though both men were actually steered by others—men like Dean Acheson for Truman and Dick Cheney for Bush, who flattered them while pulling the strings that worked them). Henry Wallace, who was the secretary of commerce when Truman became president, wrote in his 1945 diary, after a meeting with Truman:

> He also seemed eager to make decisions of every kind with the greatest promptness. Everything he said was decisive. It almost seemed as though he was eager to decide in advance of thinking.[23]

Truman said he never lost a minute's sleep over the decision to drop the bomb on Hiroshima. Bush had the same cockiness in his attitude toward the Iraq war. When Bob Woodward asked the president if he ever had doubts about the Iraq war, Bush answered:

> "I haven't suffered doubt."
> "Is that right?" I asked. "Not at all?"
> "No. And I'm able to convey that to the people."[24]

He also told Woodward, "I'm a gut player."[25] "Gut" had for him much the same meaning as "animal instincts" had for Benito Mussolini, who said:

"You must all understand that I am not to be contradicted, because it only raises doubts in my mind and diverts me from what I know to be the right path, whereas my own animal instincts are always right."[26]

When Woodward asked Bush if he ever consulted his father, the former president, for advice, Bush told him: "You know, he is the wrong father to appeal to in terms of strength. There is a higher father that I appeal to."[27] He felt very near to God—or to Billy Graham, which could be much the same thing. He claimed he had a born-again experience under Graham's guidance, which helped him overcome an addiction to alcohol. Asked in the Iowa presidential debate of January 15, 2000, for his favorite philosopher, he answered, "Christ, because he changed my heart." Asked for the source of his certitude in launching and conducting the war in Iraq, he said that he felt God had put him in office at this time to do this work.[28] He puzzled foreign leaders, like France's Jacques Chirac, while trying to recruit them as allies, by talking of the End Time.[29]

So Iraq was a war with secular outlines filled in by religious certitude. This seems like getting the worst of both worlds, bringing religious zeal to the support of a secular project. Asked about his loathing for Kim Jong Il of North Korea, Bush said, "Maybe it's my religion."[30] He also said that prayer was his main guide during the Iraq war. God and gut seemed to be jostling against each other for the war's responsibility. Since it is hard to get an exact definition of his God, we may have to settle for Douglas Feith's awed description of what it was like to go with the Bush gut:

> Expertise is a very good thing, but it is not the same thing as sound judgment regarding strategy and policy. George W. Bush has more insight, because of his knowledge of human

beings and his sense of history, about the motive force, the craving for freedom and participation in self-rule, than do many of the language experts and history experts and culture experts.[31]

NOTES

1. Lucretius, *De Rerum Natura* 1.101.
2. See the contributions of Daniel Bell, Fred Iklé, Herman Kahn, and Anthony J. Wiener in *Toward the Year 2000: Work in Progress* (MIT Press, 1996), based on the special 400-page issue of *Daedalus* (Summer 1967), especially pp. 73–122, 328–38.
3. See the American Academy of Arts and Sciences study for the year 2000, referenced immediately above.
4. The Fundamentalism Project's findings were published by the University of Chicago Press in six volumes from 1991 to 1995, edited by the project's directors, Martin E. Marty and R. Scott Appleby.
5. Martin E. Marty and R. Scott Appleby, eds., *The Fundamentalism Project*, vol. 5, *Fundamentalisms Comprehended* (University of Chicago Press, 1995), p. 441.
6. Samuel Huntington, *The Clash of Civilizations and the Remaking of World Order* (Simon & Schuster, 1996), p. 97.
7. Olivier Roy, *Holy Ignorance: When Religion and Culture Part Ways*, trans. Ros Schwartz (Oxford University Press, 2013), pp. 2–4.
8. Ibid., p. 10.
9. Molly Worthen, *Apostles of Reason: The Crisis of Authority in American Evangelicalism* (Oxford University Press, 2014), pp. 28–31, 84–87, 220–22, 258–61.
10. Michael Walzer, *The Paradox of Liberation: Secular Revolutions and Religious Counterrevolutions* (Yale University Press, 2015), p. 16.
11. Ibid., p. 27. A similar point is made by Huntington, op. cit., pp. 98–101, and by Scott L. Montgomery and Daniel Chirot, *The Shape of the New* (Princeton University Press, 2015), pp. 388–93.
12. Murray Kempton, "From the Depths of the Thirties," review of *The Unpossessed, New Republic,* Nov. 5, 1966.
13. Walzer, op. cit., p. 14.
14. Senator Lindsey Graham, speaking on the *Hugh Hewitt Show*, Jan. 7, 2015.
15. *Journal* Staff, "Scott Walker's Campaign Lets Stand 'Handful of Reasonable' Muslims Remark," *Wisconsin State Journal*, Aug. 23, 2015.

16. Stoyan Zaimov, "Obama Has 'Undying Support' for Muslims," *Christian Post*, Feb. 10, 2015.

17. Colin Campbell, "CNN's Jake Tapper to Donald Trump," CNN, Mar. 10, 2016.

18. MJ Lee, "Republicans Clash—with Civility—at Final Debate Before Decisive Contests," CNN Politics, Mar. 11, 2016.

19. I know about this because a university once assigned my *Lincoln at Gettysburg* as the entry reading, and invited me to talk with the students, some of whom asked me to sign their copies to their parents who had read it with them.

20. See the thorough discussion of the North Carolina lawsuit (*Yacovelli v. Moeser*) by Christopher Buck, "The Constitutionality of Teaching Islam: The University of North Carolina Qur'an Controversy," in *Observing the Observer: The State of Islamic Studies in American Universities*, ed. Mumtaz Ahmad, Zahid Bukhari, and Sulayman Nyang (International Institute of Islamic Thought, 2012), pp. 137–77.

21. Buck, op. cit., pp. 158–61.

22. William F. Buckley, Jr., "Are We Owed an Apology," Universal Press Syndicate, Aug. 19, 2002.

23. Henry Wallace diary, quoted by Murray Kempton, *Rebellions, Perversities, and Main Events* (Times Books, 1994), p. 425.

24. Bob Woodward, *Plan of Attack* (Simon & Schuster, 2004), p. 420.

25. Bob Woodward, *Bush at War* (Simon & Schuster, 2002), p. 137.

26. Denis Mack Smith, *Mussolini's Roman Empire* (Viking, 1976), p. 85.

27. Woodward, *Plan of Attack*, p. 421.

28. Jean Edward Smith, *Bush* (Simon & Schuster, 2016), p. 236.

29. Kurt Eichenwald, *500 Days: Secrets and Lies in the Terror Wars* (Touchstone, 2012), pp. 458–60.

30. Woodward, *Bush at War*, p. 340.

31. Jeffrey Goldberg, "A Little Learning: What Douglas Feith Knew, and When He Knew It," *New Yorker*, May 9, 2005.

CHAPTER 3

Fearful Ignorance

The total destruction of both towers of the World Trade Center, with a simultaneous attack on the Pentagon and (perhaps) on the Capitol—these stunned America as nothing else had since Pearl Harbor. Fear is rarely a good guide. The first impulse when disaster strikes is to run around, as the saying goes, like a chicken with its head cut off. Just when the head is most needed, it is the hardest thing to find. President Roosevelt, struggling for calm during the Great Depression, wisely counseled that "the only thing we have to fear is fear itself." Yet even he yielded to fear after Pearl Harbor, consigning a hundred thousand loyal Japanese Americans to concentration camps, expropriating their property, and denying them court procedures.

It is not surprising, then, that after the 9/11 attacks, we took ill-considered measures. We spied on everyone, beginning with ourselves. We looked for a country to invade, and invaded the wrong one. We cobbled together a totally new organization of security agencies. Our guard was up against all threats, known or unknown, real or imaginary. Since terrorists can strike anywhere, we had to look for them everywhere. Only governmental omniscience could protect us. To get at suspected terrorists' plans, the Office of Legal Counsel in the Justice Department, guided by David Addington in Vice President Cheney's office, authorized torture for the first time in our history. Some of the torturing we "outsourced" to secret detention centers around the world. Some we conducted ourselves in Abu Ghraib, Guantánamo, and Camp Bucca. Attorney General John Mitchell called the crimes of Watergate the "White House horrors." They were nothing compared with the White House horrors of Dick Cheney and David Addington. Cheney tried to block the anti-torture bill sponsored by Senator John McCain. When he failed to do that, Addington wrote the signing statement by which President Bush signaled his unwillingness to enforce the law.[1]

The ambitious Patriot Act, drafted immediately after 9/11, was passed by the House in a month, passed by the Senate the next day, and signed by the president on the day after that. Some of its provisions were later declared unconstitutional by various courts. In this it resembled the hasty Alien and Sedition Acts of 1798, drafted to punish people supposedly infected by sympathy with the French Revolution. In some ways the Patriot Act went beyond the 1798 legislation, allowing indefinite detention of aliens on secret evidence. It also allowed warrantless searches in the form of National Security Letters. These had to be amended by later legislation to avoid court rulings of unconstitutionality.

Another effect of panic is to throw great amounts of money at a problem. The money offered to states and cities that alleged anti-terrorist motives for new projects led to many token programs. But the real anti-terrorist measures were also stumbling over themselves—proliferating at a rate that made it hard for each improvised entity to learn what the others were doing. The *Washington Post* had an investigative team work two years just trying to track down all the programs (1,271 of them) that sprouted up throughout the government.

The new security programs were housed in thirty-three new buildings in the Washington area. In McLean, Virginia, alone, the Office of the Director of National Intelligence and the National Counterterrorism Center shared a secretive compound where 1,700 federal employees and 1,200 private contractors were working by 2010. These entities tried (and still try) to analyze a deluge of facts, near facts, plausible rumors, and time-wasting distractions. The *Washington Post* concluded, from its study, that this network "has become so large, so unwieldy, and so secretive that no one knows how much money it costs, how many people it employs, how many programs exist within it or exactly how many agencies do the same work."[2]

The panic right after 9/11 is understandable, but one might expect that a calmer way of dealing with the danger would gradually assert itself. We were knocked off balance by a sudden blow, but we should have struggled back to some degree of calm in subsequent months and years. After all, even in the first days of shock, there was a recognition that all Muslims could not be held responsible for this atrocity. President Bush made that clear when he visited a mosque just six days after 9/11. He said there that reports of Muslim women being harassed because they wore a hijab were disgraceful:

> Some don't want to go shopping for their families; some don't want to go about their ordinary daily routines because, by wearing cover, they're afraid they'll be intimidated. That should not and that will not stand in America. Those who feel like they can intimidate our fellow citizens to take out their anger don't represent the best of America, they represent the worst of humankind, and they should be ashamed of that kind of behavior. . . . They [American Muslims] love America just as much as I do.[3]

The mosque Bush went to that day was dedicated forty-four years earlier by President Eisenhower; and it would be visited fifteen years later by President Obama. Obama quoted there Thomas Jefferson's explanation of his Virginia Statute for Religious Freedom, that it was "meant to comprehend, within the mantle of its protection, the Jew and the Gentile, the Christian and Mahometan, the Hindoo, and Infidel of every denomination."[4] Obama noted that "Thomas Jefferson's opponents tried to stir things up by suggesting he was a Muslim—so I was not the first."[5] This brought laughter from its audience, but by 2016 accusations of Muslimism were no longer light things. Obama mentioned that two girls of the mosque where he was speaking had been threatened as Muslim terrorists. Mosques were regularly being denounced and vandalized. The effort to build a Muslim study center two blocks from the World Trade Center site—though it was sponsored by a Sufi (mystical) imam, Feisal Abdul Rauf, long known for his ecumenical work with other faiths—became a hotly criticized project, and was defeated.

Terrorism is a real threat, and fears of it were rightly reanimated by acts like the Boston Marathon bombing (2013) and the mass murders in San Bernardino (2015). But fear of Islam had been mounting steadily even apart from these incitements. What can explain this steady growth in anti-Muslim sentiment, when immediately after 9/11 it was so low? The sociologist Christopher Bail argues that it was because fringe groups attacking Islam displaced mainline groups speaking for the majority of Muslims in the media and on the Internet. He shows that this is true statistically. The fringe critics of Islam became newsworthy, more talked about than the mainstream organizations that were a previous source of information. Representatives of the majority Muslim culture—groups like CAIR—were shoved aside to make room for critics like Pamela

Geller of SIOA attacking "the Ground Zero Mosque," Frank Gaffney of CSP alleging Muslim infiltration of the government, Daniel Pipes of MEF saying campuses are teaching Islam, David Yerushalmi of SANE finding Shari'ah sneaking into American courts, Brigitte Gabriel of ACT saying that Islam fosters a hate for Jews and Christians, and Robert Spencer of Jihad Watch calling for a ban on the Qur'an.[6] Of course, the personnel and funds of these anti-Muslim groups have been interconnected in various ways at various times. Yerushalmi, for instance, was the lawyer for Geller in her fight against the Muslim center near the World Trade Center and got funds from Gaffney for his war on Shari'ah.[7]

Bail may give the false impression that these organizations were the main or real cause of opposition to Islam. They were probably as much the effect as the cause of a wider national fear. What caused that fear? In a word, war. War, as Clausewitz argued, tends of itself to become total because of a reciprocal "ratcheting-up" (*Wechselwirkung*) of hostilities.[8] In order to mobilize reaction to war conditions, threats from the foe must be emphasized, stating or overstating the peril—which prompts any foe, actual or potential, to respond in kind. When hostilities occur, no matter who commits them, they are often attributed to an entire body of adversaries, which may not even have known about them. When American politicians declare that ours must be holy war against Islam, even friendly Muslim Americans begin to fear their own country. And when rogue American contractors in Iraq committed war crimes, these were taken by Iraqis to be the expression of an American hatred of Islam. When Donald Trump, campaigning to be president, said that tortures greater than waterboarding are to be used against Muslims, or said that all Muslims must be barred from entering the United States, that became a great recruiting tool for ISIS, as well as a betrayal of our national principles.

Fear, no matter how justified initially, slips easily out of any restraints imposed on it. Much of the current or recent anti-Muslim animus recalls, for those of us who lived through the 1950s and 1960s, the anti-Communist hysteria of the Cold War. At that time, too, we were told that Communists or Communist sympathizers (Comsymps) had infiltrated the government, the universities, the churches. Robert Welch, the founder of the John Birch Society, thought that President Eisenhower was a Communist or the tool or dupe of the Communists—as large parts of America thought President Obama was a Muslim or a tool or a dupe of the Muslims. Enemies were skulking undetected in positions of influence. Communists were under the bed, as creeping Shari'ah is now in our legislatures. Loyalty oaths were demanded in universities then. Now Daniel Pipes of the Middle East Forum claims that over one hundred professors are apologists for Muslim terrorists.[9] Senator Joseph McCarthy said the State Department was riddled with Communist sympathizers— just as conservatives claimed that Hillary Clinton's aide Huma Abedin was infiltrating the State Department with Muslim Brotherhood doctrines.[10] In the Red Scare days, all kinds of organizations were condemned as Communist "fronts." In our time, courses taught in the Arabic language are condemned as training schools for terror.

There are differences, of course, between the anti-Communist era and our anti-Muslim days. In both periods, there was a real threat from abroad, and government intelligence agencies were right to investigate the possibility of support for the threat in our own population. But distraction from such legitimate suspicion arose from the privatizing of surveillance and denunciation—by organs like *Red Channels* in the 1950s and Campus Watch in the 2000s. Anti-Communist zeal harmed the careers and reputations of many leftists who were blacklisted in the past; but it did not create new recruits to Communism in Russia or China or countries behind the Iron Curtain. In the same way, suspicion can injure the work or lives of innocent Muslim Americans trying simply to pray or to educate their children in mosques and schools. However, the denunciation of all Muslims as terrorists does help create new enemies abroad—among Muslims who hear the anti-Muslim rantings of a Donald Trump and his millions of supporters as aimed at every believer in Islam, no matter how innocent his or her thought and activity might be. By making an enemy of their religion, we make it hard or impossible for them to support American efforts to fight the real terrorists in their parts of the world. By such indiscriminate denunciation of Muslim foes we actually create more Muslim foes.

Moreover, though technically our war on terror targets only actual terrorists, those who encourage Americans to think of it as a religious war are not only muting our message abroad but fostering religious bigotry at home. Taken in company with the "collateral damage" of citizen deaths from our attacks by land and air, we are extending the war as its focus spreads muzzily out. Who and where is the enemy? Increasingly we hear the answer, Where is it not? The hijackers of 9/11 were primarily (fifteen of the nineteen) from Saudi Arabia, but others came from the United Arab Emirates (two), Egypt (one), and Lebanon (one). They prepared themselves in Germany (Hamburg) and Afghanistan (Kabul) and the U.S. (San Diego). One place that was not connected with 9/11 is Iraq. It was thought sin enough for that country to be ruled by Saddam Hussein. But our stirring of that hornet's nest has spread the recruiting area for new terrorists throughout the world. It was said that the terrorists had to be crushed in Iraq before they could come here. But people here are now being radicalized by the Internet—people like the Boston Marathon bombers. In one sense, this has more title to be called a world war than did the eponymous one that followed on Pearl Harbor.

This is a less total mobilization than that of World War II. But what it lacks in intensity it makes up for in extent. It has become the longest war in our history. World War II was fought and won in four years, and the Civil War in four and a half; but the war after

9/11 has lasted fifteen years (and continuing) and has cost more than World War I, Korea, or Vietnam. It is creeping up toward the record costs of World War II—$5 trillion. Eight years ago, according to Nobel Prize–winning economist Joseph Stiglitz, we had already incurred the commitment of $3 trillion in war costs, and that amount is growing still.[11] Better medical care on the battlefield has lowered the number of soldiers killed, but extended the care needed for a lifetime by men and women damaged in mind and/or body. The costs, largely hidden, mount precipitately.

Our enemy, in this war, is far less localizable than it was in World War II or the Cold War. It was hard enough to find and defeat an ism like Communism. Terror is a tool, not a country. Declaring a war on it is less like normal warfare, country versus country. It is more like the War on Poverty or the War on Drugs. These have often seemed wars on phantoms, fought with tools randomly or overly used, getting results hyped as promising or intended to encourage further effort, with strong lunges in wrong directions justified by consolatory gestures, as cash evanesces into the indiscernible. There is no VE Day or VJ Day in such wars.

Living with fear is corrosive. It depletes the patience to sort out threats and to calibrate responses. The less we know about the reality of Islam, the more we will fight shadows and false emanations from our own apprehension. Ignorance is the natural ally of fear. It is time for us to learn about the real Islam, beginning with its source book, the Qur'an.

NOTES

1. Barton Gellman, *Angler: The Cheney Vice Presidency* (Viking, 2008), pp. 299–323.
2. Dana Priest and William M. Arkin, "A Hidden World, Growing Beyond Control," *Washington Post*, July 19, 2010.

3. "Remarks by the President at Islamic Center of Washington, D.C.," White House Press Office, Sept. 17, 2001.

4. For Jefferson's attitude toward Muslims, see Denise A. Spellberg, *Thomas Jefferson's Qur'an: Islam and the Founders* (Vintage Books, 2013), especially p. 119. Keith Ellison, elected to Congress from Minnesota in 2006, borrowed Jefferson's Qur'an from the Library of Congress for use at his swearing-in (Spellberg, pp. 284–87). The second Muslim to enter the House, Andre Carson, used the United States Constitution, instead of either the Bible or the Qur'an, for his swearing-in. See Talib I. Karim, "Second Muslim Taking His Seat in the House of Representatives," *Muslim Link,* Apr. 1, 2008.

5. White House Press Office, Feb. 2, 2016.

6. Christopher Bail, *Terrified: How Anti-Muslim Fringe Organizations Became Mainstream* (Princeton University Press, 2015), especially pp. 114–21. To keep the players straight:

> CAIR = Council on American Islamic Relations
> SIOA = Stop the Islamization of America
> CSP = Center for Security Policy
> MEF = Middle East Forum
> SANE = Society of Americans for National Existence
> ACT = ACT for America

7. Andrea Elliott, "The Man Behind the Anti-Shariah Movement," *New York Times,* July 30, 2011.

8. Carl von Clausewitz, *Vom Kriege* 1.1.3.

9. "'Campus Watch' Lists 108 Academics Supporting Apologists for Terrorism," Middle East Forum, Oct. 21, 2002.

10. Jason Linkins, "Michele Bachmann Points to Huma Abedin as Muslim Brotherhood Infiltrator," *Huffington Post,* July 19, 2012.

11. Joseph E. Stiglitz and Linda J. Bilmes, *The Three Trillion Dollar War: The True Cost of the Iraq Conflict* (W. W. Norton, 2008).

Part II

The Qur'an: Searching *for* Knowledge

CHAPTER 4

A Desert Book

The Qur'an is haunted by something omnipresent, but only implicitly—the Arabian desert. It is always there, always in the background. One finds it in the yearning, everywhere, toward water—water as a symbol of God's blessing. Water *as* God's blessing. Water as miracle. Water creating oases. Water as reward. Water as the instrument of ritual cleansings. Water as the condition of happiness. Water as heaven. Water is even the essence of hell, where it is poured boiling down the throats of sinners.

Of course, water is important in many religions. In the Old Testament, the righteous flourish like trees along the water's edge. Yahweh, when displeased, withholds rain (Am 4.7). Pleased, he sends it. With it, he answers Elijah's prayer (1 Kgs 18.42–45). Through it Elisha cures the leper (2 Kgs 5.14). Rain brings on the rainbow (Gn 9.17). God parts the Red Sea water for Moses to pass through. He makes water spring from the rock when Moses strikes it (Num 20.11). It is used for ritual cleansing in mikvehs.

In the New Testament, Jesus promises to give believers an endless inner spring of "living water" (Jn 4.10–13). He works a miracle though the waters in the pool of Siloam (Jn 9.7). He is baptized in it, and others become his followers by being baptized in it.

But water, always important, is insistently more so in the Arabian desert, which makes it more precious than gold. It is vital in every way—actually (physically), symbolically, even theologically. As the finest material substance, it is first in the order of creation and the medium through which other things are individuated and kept alive.

Nowhere else do you get a greater feel for the benignity of rain—or of water in any form. There is a reverent sense of the blessedness of rivers. Even the water on which ships float is called a direct favor from God. That is why water reigns in the Muslim idea of heaven. In the Jewish and Christian Bibles, heaven is Zion, the city of God (Is 60.14), the heavenly Jerusalem (Heb 12.22), an urban ideal. But in the Qur'an, heaven is the oasis of oases, rinsed with sweet waters, with rivers running on it and under it, and with springs opening unbidden. When I was growing up in the 1940s, a song was everywhere on the radio, "Cool Water" sung by Vaughn Monroe. As I read the Qur'an, it keeps coming back to me, unbidden.

Rain's power to revivify starved plants in the desert is the book's favorite way to explain a part of God's message that met great resistance in Muhammad's time, the resurrection of the body. At Allah's direction, Muhammad never tires of the desert miracle, the rebirth of plants and flowers:

Another of His signs is this: you see the earth lying desolate, but when We send water down on to it, it stirs and grows. He who gives it life will certainly give life to the dead. (41.39)

He brings the living out of the dead and the dead out of the living. He gives life to the earth after death, and you will be brought out in the same way. One of His signs is that He created you from dust and—lo and behold!—you became human and scattered far and wide. . . . He sends water down

from the sky to restore the earth to life after death. There truly
are signs in this for those who use their reason. (30.19–20, 24)

Noah, as he tries to recall his people from sin, tells them to remember

"how God made you spring forth from the earth like a plant,
how He will return you into it and then bring you out again."
(71.17–18)

The life-giving quality of rain stands for something that goes
beyond itself in sheer vitality:

It is God who sends the winds, bearing good news of His
coming grace, and when they have gathered up the heavy
clouds, We drive them to a dead land where We cause rain to
fall, bringing out all kinds of crops, just as We shall bring out
the dead. (7.57)

The reanimation of earth by water repeats the creation itself.

Are the disbelievers not aware that the heavens and the earth
used to be joined together and that We ripped them apart,
that we made every living thing from water? (21.30)

and God created each animal out of [its own] fluid. (24.45)

Water is a principle of unity in source (from the One God) and of
division (into the variety of created things). As it reanimates the
flowers, it quickens dust into Adam's form:

"Have you no faith in Him who created you from dust, from
a small drop of fluid, then shaped you into a man?" (18.37)

Water is itself divided into salt water, in which fish can live and on which ships carry men and things from one place to another, and sweet water, which land creatures can drink and be nourished by:

> We send down pure water from the sky, so that We can revive a dead land with it, and We give it as a drink to many animals and people We have created. . . . It is He who released the two bodies of flowing water, one sweet and fresh and the other salty and bitter, and put an insurmountable barrier between them. It is He who creates human beings from fluid, then makes them kin by blood and marriage: your Lord is all powerful! (25.48, 53–54)

This last sentence shows how water in its various forms is the medium God uses for creation. Though Surah 4.1 gives only one source of creation, the multiplicity of things comes from water's power to variegate what comes from that source. Water is a miraculous intermediary. To a desert culture, water is not only needed for life. It *is* life. It is the material thing nearest to God. The book finds many ways to celebrate it.

> Do they [*unbelievers*] not see the sky above them—how We have built and adorned it, with no rifts in it; how We spread out the earth and put firm mountains on it, and caused every kind of joyous plant to grow in it, as a lesson and reminder for every servant who turns to God; and how We send blessed water down from the sky and grow with it gardens, the harvest grain, and tall palm trees laden with clusters of dates, as a provision for everyone; how with water We give [new] life to a land that is dead? This is how the dead will emerge [from their graves]. (50.6–11)

He restores the earth to life after death: this same God is the
One who will return people to life after death. (30.50)

It is God who sends forth the winds; they raise up the clouds;
We drive them to a dead land [*the desert*] and with them revive
the earth after its death; such will be the Resurrection. (35.9)

Since water is so precious in the desert, knowing your way to
water, to the next oasis, is a survival skill. The standard of a moral
life is that one stays on a path. That is true of Jewish and Christian
uses of path as a moral term, the path of righteousness. In the Gospel of John (14.6), Jesus says, "I am The Path [Hē Hodos], and The
Truth, and The Life. No one can reach the Father but by way of me."
In the Acts of the Apostles, Christianity itself is called simply The
Path (Hē Hodos). Saul, before becoming Paul, persecutes "followers
of The Path" (9.2, 22.4), but after his conversion he follows The Path
(24.14). Converts were catechized in The Path (18.25–26). Nonbe-
lievers attack The Path (19.9, 23), though a Roman procurator was
lenient toward The Path (24.22).

Though many speak of morality as following "the straight and
narrow path," this language has a special meaning in the desert
culture of the Qur'an, whose opening prayer is "Guide us to the
straight path" (1.6). Knowing and keeping to a sure and quick path
was used for getting to water, to the next oasis. The one who knows
what this route is and can lead others on it holds the key to life or
death. If one does not reach water in a timely way, one can wander
and die of all the ills brought on by dehydration. Allah's great
mercy is shown in the fact that he gives people a sure path.

Now We have set you [Muhammad] on a clear religious path
[*shari'ah*], so follow it. Do not follow the desires of those who
lack [true] knowledge. (45.18)

Joseph E. B. Lumbard glosses this aya in *The Study Quran* this way:

> In this context *clear path* translates *shari'ah*, which later became the technical term for Islamic Law, though it occurs only this one time in the Quran. Linguistically, shari'ah means a straight, smooth path that leads to water, which in the deserts of Arabia would also have meant a path to salvation from death. (SQ 1220)

Knowing how and where to reach water was essential not only to physical survival but to spiritual health, since water was required for all the ritual oblations required in the Qur'an. Water not only vivifies; it purifies. Since one cannot pray in an unclean state, and must first be cleansed, what will happen to a party that is still far from an oasis but needs to pray? The only option is to take the finest cleanest sand and perform a kind of ablution by gentle abrasion. As Gibbon put it:

> Cleanliness is the key of prayer: the frequent lustration of the hands, the face, and the body, which was practised of old by the Arabs, is solemnly enjoined by the Koran; and a permission is formally granted to supply with sand the scarcity of water.[1]

This problem is addressed twice in the Qur'an:

> You who believe, do not come anywhere near the prayer if you are intoxicated, not until you know what you are saying; nor if you are in a state of major ritual impurity—though you may pass through the mosque—not until you have bathed; if you are ill, on a journey, have relieved yourselves, or had intercourse,

and cannot find any water, then find some clean sand and wipe your faces and hands with it. God is always ready to pardon and forgive. (4.43)

You who believe, when you are about to pray, wash your faces and your hands and arms up to the elbows, wipe your heads, wash your feet up to the ankles and, if required, wash your whole body. If any of you is sick or on a journey, or has just relieved himself, or had intimate contact with a woman, and can find no water, then take some clean sand and wipe your face and hands with it. God does not wish to place any burden on you; He only wishes to cleanse you and perfect His blessing on you, so that you may be thankful. (5.6)

In a particularly trying situation—as when Muhammad's troops were trapped by superior numbers before the Battle of Badr—Allah may send a strengthening sleep and purifying rain to his protected followers, giving not only sustenance but purification:

Remember when He gave you sleep as a reassurance from Him, and sent down water from the sky to cleanse you, to remove Satan's pollution from you, to make your hearts strong and your feet firm. (8.11)

"Water from the sky" means water sent not from clouds but direct from God—as we speak of "a bolt out of the blue" (lightning not coming from storm cloud). It is a blessing like the manna rained upon the Israelites. Everyone with Muhammad is bathed in this sacramental water.

The deathly nature of the desert without water is suggested when Muhammad throws sand at the army arrayed against him.

Muhammad's troops are miraculously rained upon, while the enemy is left to perish in waterless desert:

> It was not you who killed them but God, and when you [Prophet] threw [sand at them] it was not your throw [that defeated them] but God's, to do the believers a favour: God is all seeing and all knowing—"That is what you get!"—and God will weaken the disbelievers' designs. (8.17–18)

A particularly harsh curse against a foe is that "its water may sink so deep into the ground that you will never be able to reach it again" (18.41).

Moses leads the Israelites through a waterless wilderness for three days and they are crying for water, when he finds the oasis at Marah—but its waters are undrinkably brackish until Moses, directed by God, throws in a purifying log (Ex 15.22–25). Later, Moses strikes a rock, and water pours from it (Ex 17.6—cf. Num 20.8–11). The parallels between Moses leading Israel through the wilderness and Muhammad leading his followers through the desert are frequent and deliberate, but the Qur'an is more haunted by desert culture than the Old Testament is. All moral striving in the Qur'an is along a path whose goal is water in abundance, where everything is purified by never-failing waters. The water of Moses is vivifying, but the water of the Qur'an is also purifying.

All created things are signs in the Qur'an, but water has the most significances. It is a kind of grace, or foretaste of the rinsed-pure haven that is the Muslim's final reward, the place where all things recover their original purity, their glow. Moses is given a foretaste of what heaven might mean in the mysterious and mystic Surah 18 (a favorite of Sufi Islamism), where Moses takes his young servant (*fata*), traditionally known as Joshua, to find where the archetypal two bodies of water meet, the salt one and the fresh one. These have different powers in the temporal world. The salt water serves for humans to cross between continents, to communicate and bring supplies to each other. But people can only cross such water if they are carrying sweet water with them along with land food. They can, by contrast, live continuously on land, where there is sweet water. In heaven, there will be a supernaturally sweet water, and no salt water at all.

These two basic waters are, in their essence, divided by an insurmountable barrier: "They meet, yet there is a barrier between them they do not cross" (55.19–20—cf. 25.53, 27.61). Where they ultimately meet, they keep their own nature—like oil and water, they remain separate no matter how mingled. This intermediate but incommensurable stage is called the *barzakh,* and it is used for the state of the soul as it crosses over from First Life through death to the Second Life (SQ 729, 1827–28). The *barzakh* is symbolic therefore of all the differences-in-continuity between this life's knowledge and heavenly apprehensions, or of earthly reasoning and mystical wisdom. A person's life must change to enter the afterlife, but it must remain the same person's, to be credited with all the faults or blessings incurred on earth.

Moses and his *fata,* in Surah 18, have set out to find the meeting place of the two water systems. We are not directly told what Moses's motive is in this quest, but we can deduce it from instructions given Moses—not to try to know or pretend to know more than is human. It is clear that he was trying to get a peek into the afterlife—in effect, trying to explore the *barzakh* before it was his proper time to die. He and his companion, failing to find the meeting place of the waters, sit down at a rock to rest. Then they get up and travel on, till Moses asks for the fish they brought with them to eat. The *fata* says that Satan made him forget to tell Moses that the fish, revivified, had swum off from their resting spot (18.62–63). Moses recognizes that this had to be the *barzakh,* if a dead fish came to life again and swam off in the waters of the afterlife. That spot was where they could get a glimpse of the world beyond this. A little parting of the veil had occurred there, and they had missed it. They must hurry back to look again.

But when they get back they encounter a mysterious wise man (apparently an angel or a righteous jinni).[2] They would like to follow him, to acquire his wisdom; but he says they must never question what he does or says. Moses breaks that command when his guide does outrageous things—punches a hole in a boat, kills a child, repairs a wall without pay (18.71–82). The acts and words resemble Zen koans, and Moses will not understand them in this life. All he has learned is that when he really (not just in vision) goes through the *barzakh,* he will be following the resuscitated fish that slipped away from him into miraculous waters.

I should not leave the subject of desert culture without mentioning the great need it created for the most serviceable instrument in the desert, the camel. The Qur'an's most vivid picture of the end of the world begins this way:

> When the sun is rolled up, when the stars are dimmed, when the mountains are set in motion, when pregnant camels are abandoned . . . (81.1–4)

The dearest possession, about to bring forth another valuable property, will no longer matter when the apocalypse is here. Joseph Lumbard explains why this is such a terrible omen of disaster in the desert:

> Pregnant camels translates *ishar,* which is said to indicate the best type of camel when it has reached the tenth month of pregnancy. Camels were central to Arabian livelihood, and a pregnant camel would thus have been a salient metaphor for

the Arabs of the time, indicating that on the Day of Judgment people will be so preoccupied with their immediate state that they will have no concern for wealth, even their most precious property. (SQ 1480)

Gibbon understood the lifesaving power of a camel in the desert:

> In the sands of Afric and Arabia, the camel is a sacred and precious gift. That strong and patient beast of burthen can perform, without eating or drinking, a journey of several days; and a reservoir of fresh water is preserved in a large bag, a fifth stomach of the animal, whose body is imprinted with the marks of servitude: the larger breed is capable of transporting a weight of a thousand pounds; and the dromedary, of a lighter and more active frame, outstrips the fleetest courser in the race. Alive or dead, almost every part of the camel is serviceable to man: her milk is plentiful and nutritious; the young and tender flesh has the taste of veal: a valuable salt is extracted from the urine: the dung supplies the deficiency of fuel; and the long hair, which falls each year and is renewed, is coarsely manufactured into the garments, the furniture, and the tents, of the Bedoweens.[3]

Watery Heaven

The right path leads on earth to the Zamzam well in Mecca, which formed the oasis with the holy ground of the Ka'bah. Zamzam sprang up, according to Muslims' sacred lore, when the baby Ishmael, Abraham's son by Hagar and the ancestor of Muhammad, cried from thirst and the well opened up for him.[4] It is still a part of the hajj, the great pilgrimage, to drink from the waters of

Zamzam. But even this holy water is just a foretaste of the oasis of all oases—heaven, which is called the Gardens.

In the Qur'an, as in Genesis, life for Adam and Eve begins in a pleasant garden. But after they disobey God, they are expelled into the desert, where they will be tested again. If they and their descendants accept God's guidance, they will return to the Garden of Gardens, which is in every way the opposite of the desert they were stranded in during life.

> "In the garden you will never go hungry, feel naked, *be thirsty, or suffer the heat of the sun.*" (20.118–19, emphasis added)

Heaven is a place where water can never be wanted.

> God has promised the believers, both men and women, Gardens graced with flowing streams where they will remain. (9.72)

> These will have the reward of the [true] home: they will enter perpetual Gardens, along with their righteous ancestors, spouses, and descendants; the angels will go in to them from every gate, "Peace be with you, because you have remained steadfast. What an excellent reward is this home of yours!" (13.22–24)

> He will forgive your sins, admit you into Gardens graced with flowing streams, into pleasant dwellings in the Gardens of Eternity. (61.12)

When water miracles occur in life, it is like a momentary breaking in of heaven on earth. When Mary the mother of Jesus is suffering in childbirth, a voice comes to her promising an instant oasis just tailored to her needs:

"Do not worry: your Lord has *provided a stream at your feet* and, if you shake the trunk of the palm tree towards you, it will deliver fresh ripe dates for you." (19.24–25, emphasis added)

Heaven in the Qur'an is not rinsed and purified only by wells and rivers. There are springs and water under the earth.

A drink will be passed round among them from a flowing spring. (37.45)

Heaven is a glorified version of the oases that Arabs found in the desert. The high water table at those earthly spots not only fed the palm trees and other vegetation but ensured that rain, when it occured, would not be drained at once into the sand.

Those who believed and did good deeds will be brought into Gardens graced with flowing streams, there to remain with their Lord's permission: their greeting there is "Peace." (14.23)

They will have not only a sufficiency of water there, but an eternal surplus:

We have put gardens of date palms and grapes in the earth, and We have made springs of water gush out of it. (36.34)

In the heavenly garden there is never-ending water to hand. In fact, one has only to wish for it and a spring will appear.

We shall have removed all ill feeling from their hearts; streams will flow at their feet. (7.43)

The righteous will have a drink mixed with *kafur* [*fragrant herb*], a spring from which God's servants drink, making it flow plentifully. (76.5–6)

As water is the source of differentiation among earthly creatures, it provides in heaven's springs a kind of superwater that is better than any water loved in the desert.

Here is a picture of the Garden promised to the pious: rivers of water forever pure, rivers of milk forever fresh, rivers of wine, a delight for those who drink, rivers of honey clarified and pure, [all] flow in it; there they will find fruit of every kind; and they will find forgiveness from their Lord. (47.15)

How can the Muslims be promised wine in heaven when they are forbidden to drink it on earth? All the liquids in heaven are supernatural, not the sort known in a prior life. The "forever fresh" milk, springing from the earth, is cowless and never goes sour. The honey, without the impurities of wax combs, is beeless. The wine is a superwine that does not muddle the head. It "causes no headache or intoxication" (56.19). Everything in the Gardens is supernatural, not subject to any uncleanness of their degraded likeness on earth.

The Qur'an is inventive in all the ways it describes heaven as the anti-desert. In the desert, shade is rare, always sought, at times—or often—not found. In heaven, it is everywhere:

We shall admit them into cool refreshing shade. (4.57)

On earth, shade is only in some places and at some times, but in heaven it is "perpetual" (13.35), in all directions (56.30), always over the spouses (36.56), protecting them from the "scorching heat" of the desert (76.13). This shade is preternatural. It does not come from cloud cover. In the desert, clouds were rare and welcome, because they might bear rain. The winds, which can blow in clouds, are praised as a mercy of God ten times in the Qur'an (SQ 1058).

It is God who sends forth the winds; they raise up the clouds;
We drive them to a dead land and with them revive the earth
after its death. (35.9)

Since there is no more death in heaven, there is no need of the symbolic resurrection from death that was "the sign" of rain on earth. Water does not rain down in heaven. It wells up endlessly in rivulets, fountains, springs, and wells. Water had to be brought to earth in the desert, life brought to death. In heaven, life flows from the earth, life where there is no death. The heaven of the Qur'an, with its crystalline celestial bodies, is a kind of theological science fiction. That was the point of Moses's vision as he sought the meeting point of two waters (earthly and heavenly). The wise guide who spoke to him used what seems like the Lewis Carroll upside-down logic of Wonderland. But this is a topsy-turvydom where a higher wisdom sees the need for scuttling a boat, killing a child, or gratuitously upholding a wall. Heaven's ways are not reachable with earth's limited knowledge. Moses is forbidden to equate the two. In heaven, everything is *totaliter aliter* (totally not-like).

Hell

In the Qur'an, there are dozens of descriptions of the watery cool Gardens, but they mainly just repeat the same themes.[5] There are far more descriptions—hundreds of them—devoted to the penalties that will be inflicted on sinners in hell. If heaven gives respite from the desert, hell just intensifies all its worst aspects—fierce heat, deep thirst, hallucinations of relief. Some have represented

Islam as a hedonistic religion; it is actually an ascetic one, a fasting one, a fearful one. No Puritan preacher of hellfire, not Jonathan Edwards himself, can outdo the terrors described in the Qur'an. A desert thirst is still there, but the only water to drink is boiling water. The damned keep trying to drink it because the only thing they have to eat is a bitter fruit, *zaqqum*, that increases thirst.

> Is this [*the Gardens*] the better welcome, or the tree of Zaqqum, which We have made a test for the evildoers? This tree grows in the heart of the blazing Fire, and its fruits are like devils' heads. They will fill their bellies eating from it; then drink a scalding mixture on top of it; then return to the blazing Fire. (37.62–68)

They go from the destructive food back to the boiling water that tears up their insides. No camel, with its great storage capacity for water, ever drank more when it finally reached an oasis than these thirst-driven people must keep drinking in their folly (56.92–93). Boiling water pours down their throats as molten gold is poured down the gullets of misers in medieval Christian frescoes of hell.

On their bodies, the sinners of the Qur'an have garments of fire; it is a clothing they carry everywhere with them. When they run from the fire, they are driven back by a more intense fire. These passages remind me of the way Ruskin sees Ulysses in Dante's *Inferno,* with "the restless flame in which he is wrapt continually . . . [a] waving garment of torture, which quivers as he speaks, and aspires as he moves."[6]

Vivid as these descriptions of physical sufferings are, the psychological punishments are subtler but deeper. Self-alienation is the penalty for self-aggrandizement. The sinners are turned against themselves. Their very skin, the thing that feels the fire most immediately, testifies against them. The sinner wanted to use the skin for

lust and luxury; it now tells the owner of that skin that it was mis-
used. It was not the skin's fault, and it is now telling its user that he
should not have involved it for evil purposes.

> On the Day when God's enemies are gathered up for the Fire
> and driven onward, their ears, eyes, and skins will, when they
> reach it, testify against them for their misdeeds. They will say
> to their skins, "Why did you testify against us?" and their
> skins will reply, "God, who gave speech to everything, has
> given us speech—it was He who created you the first time
> and to Him you have been returned—yet you did not try to hide
> yourselves from your ears, eyes, and skin to prevent them from
> testifying against you. You thought that God did not know
> about much of what you were doing, so it was the thoughts you
> entertained about your Lord that led to your ruin, and you
> became losers." (41.19–23)

> Today We seal up their mouths, but their hands speak to
> Us, and their feet bear witness to everything they have done.
> (36.65)

The tongue, once used to deceive, seduce, or lie, now returns to its
proper work, telling the truth about its owner. All parts were created to serve God. The innocent parts say they were not partners in
the evildoing that took place in the mind's direction of them. They
were captive to their owner's attempt at rebellion. One part of the
self tried to conscript them, but they protest their own misuse.

NOTES

1. Edward Gibbon, *The History of the Decline and Fall of the Roman Empire*, ed.
   David Womersley (Penguin, 1994), vol. 3, p. 185.

2. Though jinn generally make trouble for humans, some—like Solomon's adjutants at 27.17, SQ 931—perform good deeds for them.
3. Gibbon, op. cit., p. 155.
4. Jonathan A. C. Brown, *Muhammad: A Very Short Introduction* (Oxford University Press, 2011), p. 4.
5. See 16.31, 18.31, 20.76, 61.12, 98.8.
6. John Ruskin, *The Works of John Ruskin*, vol. 22, lecture 4, ed. E. T. Cook and Alexander Wetterburn (George Allen, 1906), pp. 176–77.

CHAPTER 5

Conversing with the Cosmos

Sinners in hell are tortured by their own body parts—speaking body parts. When the sinner asks his own skin how it can talk, skin answers him: "God, who gave speech to everything, has given us speech" (41.21). Other things also speak. Birds talk. So do ants. So do mountains and stars.

> Solomon succeeded David. He said, "People, we have been taught the speech of birds, and we have been given a share of everything: this is clearly a great favour." Solomon's hosts of jinn, men, and birds were marshalled in ordered ranks before him, and when they came to the Valley of the Ants, one ant said, "Ants! Go into your homes, in case Solomon and his hosts unwittingly crush you." (27.16–18)

Saint Francis is said to have preached to the birds. In the Qur'an, birds preach—or at least bring information—to Solomon. A particularly talkative bird in the Qur'an is the variously dappled hoopoe (a favorite bird of Aristophanes). Just when Solomon is about to punish the hoopoe for not showing up at inspection time, the bird flits in with a news flash. The hoopoe is a spy for Solomon, who will forgive the bird's tardiness if its information is confirmed. Here is the hoopoe's lengthy report:

> "I have learned something you did not know: I come to you from Sheba with firm news. I found a woman ruling over the people, who has been given a share of everything—she has a magnificent throne—[but] I found that she and her people worshipped the sun instead of God. Satan has made their deeds alluring to them, and diverted them from the right path: they cannot find the right path. Should they not worship God, who brings forth what is hidden . . . and what you declare? He is God, there is no god but Him, the Lord of the mighty throne." (27.22–26)

Solomon writes a letter for the hoopoe to deliver to the people of Sheba (27.27–28), which obviously involves some more converse with his bird—who is surely the Chatty Cathy of this aviary. The raven of Surah 5 does not speak when he shows Adam's bad son how to bury the body of the brother he murdered (5.31)—but all things somehow or other signal the will of their maker. Similarly, the trained birds of Abraham fly back to him when he calls them from far-off hills, showing how God can restore separated body parts to one life (2.260).

The loquacious hoopoe and demonstrative raven and trained birds may seem to belong more to the world of folktales than of scripture; but all things talk in the Qur'an. It is abuzz with conversation. For Allah, the real meaning of creating is communicating. The Qur'an is an exercise in semiotics. God speaks a special language, in which mountains and winds and springs are the syllables. Everything is a sign. Even the light is just a pointer to a light beyond light. God's light shines through everything, including every lower light:

> God is the light of the heavens and earth. His Light is like this [*parable*]: there is a niche, and in it a lamp, the lamp inside a glass, a glass like a glittering star, fuelled from a blessed olive tree from neither east nor west, whose oil almost gives light even when no fire touches it—light upon light—God guides whoever He will to His Light. (24.35)

In fact, all creatures speak in a sign language about their maker.

> The seven heavens and the earth and everyone in them glorify Him. There is not a single thing that does not celebrate His praise. (17.44)

The psalmist looks to the mountains for inspiration (Ps 121.1); but in the Qur'an, mountains are fellow prophets along with David:

> We made the mountains and the birds celebrate our praises with David. (21.79)

> We graced David with Our favour. We said, "You mountains, echo God's praises together with him." (34.10)

> We made the mountains join him [*David*] in glorifying Us at sunset and sunrise. (38.18)

The close association of Moses with mountains is shown when God convinces Moses of his inscrutability by ordering a mountain to fall down, and the mountain obeys:

When his Lord revealed Himself to the mountain, He made it crumble: Moses fell down unconscious. (7.143)

This responsiveness of the creation to its Creator resembles that of the morning stars when God describes his creative activity in the Book of Job (38.6–7).

> *Whereupon are the foundations thereof fastened,*
>   *or who laid the cornerstone thereof,*
> *when the morning stars sang together,*
>   *and all the sons of God shouted for joy?*

In the New Testament, when Pharisees try to silence the followers of Jesus, he tells them, "If they are silenced, the stones would cry out of themselves" (Lk 19.40). In the Qur'an, too, stones can be demonstratively pious:

> Your hearts became as hard as rocks, or even harder, for there are rocks from which streams spring out, and some from which water comes when they split open, and others which fall down in awe of God. (2.74)

It is a common theme of monotheistic faith that God's creatures express aspects of his reality. The mountains speak of steadiness (Ps 36.6). Lilies of the field speak of trust (Mt 6.29). A corpse can speak when touched by part of a precious cow killed in sacrifice (2.72–73). God can communicate with Moses through a speaking tree:

> A voice called out to him from the right-hand side of the valley, from a tree on the blessed ground. (28.30)

Water speaks at Job 28.14, saying it does not contain wisdom:

The depths of ocean say, "It is not in us,"
And the sea says, "It is not with me."

Augustine described how this dialogue with nature leads up to communication with God. He asked the universe what and where was God.

I interrogated the earth, which replied, "It isn't me." And all things upon the earth gave the same testimony. I interrogated the sea, its depths, with their slithery live things, and they informed me, "We are not your God; seek above us." I interrogated the veering winds, but the air with its flying inhabitants said, "Anaximenes was wrong; I am not God." I interrogated the cosmos—sun, moon, stars—which said, "Nor are we that God you are searching for." So I addressed the entirety of things that impinge on the portals of my body: "Tell me about that God of mine that you are not. Tell me something about Him." And clamorous together they spoke back: "He made us." My interrogation was nothing but my yearning, and their response was nothing but their beauty.[1]

This process of searching through all the marvels of God's creation to find the creator resembles Abraham's search in the Qur'an to find the One God:

When the night grew dark over him he saw a star and said, "This is my Lord," but when it set, he said, "I do not like things that set." And when he saw the moon rising, he said,

"*This* is my Lord," but when it too set, he said, "If my Lord does not guide me, I shall be one of those who go astray." Then he saw the sun rising and cried, "*This* is my Lord! This is greater." But when the sun set, he said, "My people, I disown all that you worship beside God. I have turned my face as a true believer towards Him who created the heavens and the earth. I am not one of the polytheists." (6.76–79)

Augustine and Abraham engage the universe in dialogue. Creation is, for them both, a form of communication. If the response of the universe is mostly a silent one, even that amounts to a silent language. The universe usually does not openly talk. It needs the help of those many messengers God sends to make humankind understand what things are saying.

We offered the Trust [*Covenant*] to the heavens, the earth, and the mountains, yet they refused to undertake it and were afraid of it; mankind undertook it—they have always been very inept and rash. (33.72)[2]

The universe has what Joseph Lumbard calls a pretemporal Covenant, which is spelled out in historical forms for humans—in Torah, and Gospel, and Qur'an (SQ 1769–75). These temporal manifestations of the original Covenant are in constant communication with God, who sends streams of people to remind humankind of the Covenants, which are all one because the underwriter of them is the One. These reminders, or warners, or messengers, or prophets speak in the different languages of the message's recipients.

We have never sent a messenger who did not use his own people's language to make things clear for them. (14.4)

The Covenant was in existence from the outset, and Adam was the first to break it, though he repented and was forgiven:

> We also commanded Adam before you, but he forgot and We found him lacking in constancy. (20.115)

> Then Adam received some words from his Lord and He accepted his repentance: He is the Ever Relenting, the Most Merciful. (2.37)

If Allah sometimes seems like a nagging parent in the Qur'an, it is because he has surrounded humanity with a continual hum and buzz of messages, which are being ignored or defied. At times, he sounds exasperated and says, "Use your head! Didn't you hear me talking to you in the stars and the sea and the mountains? Didn't you get the message?" Then, above all the signaling he contrived in this talky universe, he dictated the various Covenants, obligingly put in each community's own language—Hebrew for Jews, Greek for Christians, Arabic for Muslims. On top of that, he sends a continual stream of emissaries to refresh people's memories of their own creation and that of their surroundings.

Allah demands that people should show the same regard for created things that he has. When he made the first man, Adam, he told all the angels to bow down to him:

> Then We said to the angels, "Bow down before Adam," and they did. But not Iblis [*Satan*]: he was not one of those who bowed down. God said, "What prevented you from bowing down as I commanded you?" and he said, "I am better than him: You created me from fire and him from clay." God said, "Get down from here! This is no place for your arrogance. Get out! You are contemptible." (7.11–13)[3]

Iblis is thinking of social rank, and of his own place in such a ranking. God is telling us to find God in all his creatures. In that sense, we should bow to the mountains and the sea, getting the message God sends us through them, not saying, "I am nobler than a mountain. God cannot talk to me through something inferior to me." This reminds me of a parable G. K. Chesterton wrote in the form of a mini-drama, "The Wild Knight." The knight of the title goes through the world hoping for a vision of God— and it comes to him in the villain, Orm, who kills him. He sees at last that even Orm is made in God's image. So are stars and mountains. Marilynne Robinson said that every act of creation is a form of incarnation—of God entering the material things he makes.

Chesterton said the great merit of love is that it makes one treasure another person as we should treasure all persons, all existence in its many forms, recognizing "the whole divine democracy of things."[4] One of his early love poems says:

A lady sat down to the piano
And I lit two candles, one on each side of her.
The angel of creation felt so
When he stretched forth his hands and lit
The evening and morning stars.[5]

Besides, there is another point being made when Allah orders the angels to bow down to Adam. The point is that Allah can use anything, even lower things, to teach others about himself. He can use mountains to teach men, or men to teach angels. In one explanation of the bowing-down story, God shows the angels that Adam knows something they do not—God has taught him what to call all the other earthly creatures.

He taught Adam all the names [of things], then He showed them to the angels and said, "Tell me the names of these if you truly [think you can]." They said, "May You be glorified! We have knowledge only of what You have taught us. You are the All Knowing and All Wise." (2.31–32)

What Allah criticizes in the pagan polytheism is that it clutters up, with competing local messages, the one clear wavelength he has been broadcasting on from the moment and the act of creation:

In matters of faith, He has laid down for you [people] the same commandment that He gave Noah, which We have revealed to you [Muhammad] and which We enjoined on Abraham and Moses and Jesus. (42.13)

Modern anthropologists have tended to think religious practice starts with minor tutelary gods for protection of one's own tribe or family, or for food or trade, or for victory in war. Only when the limits of competing gods are impressed on men, as gods fail or prevail against other gods, do they then hope for one "highest" to resolve the conflicts of the lesser gods. In that sense, one ascends to monotheism as a later form of culture. But Allah says there was a primordial pact for all people from one source. It is only when people tune out from that signal that they flounder around looking for some protection tailored to their petty needs. In this view, humankind begins with monotheism and only then devolves into the scramble of gods with separate little fiefdoms. Allah, by contrast, is the ruler and maker of all that has been made.

Allah says that he is not only a demanding single authority but the caretaker of all their needs, down to the hairs on believers' heads. He could even be seen as a busybody God—what Chesterton calls "that ancient Eavesdropper / Behind the starry arras of the skies."[6] For Muhammad, he even proves to be a marriage counselor, telling him how to handle squabbles among his wives (33.28–34— see chapter 11 below). Since his message is being streamed at all times, the requirement to stay tuned by constant prayer—at least five times a day—keeps up our end of the conversation. Muhammad brings Allah's word to the inner needs of believers.

This is not a distant God. Believers can hear him speaking to them through Muhammad, who "is closer to the believers than they are themselves" (33.6)—a passage that reminds me of Augustine's description of God who is "more in me than I am in me," who is "inside me while I am outside myself."[7] If we look inward on ourselves, or outward to the stars, everything speaks of him. Belief is just joining in the conversation.

NOTES

1. Augustine, *Confessions* 10.9.
2. For Trust as a synonym for Covenant, see 26.192.
3. The same story is told at 2.34, 15.31–40, 17.61–65, 18.50.
4. G. K. Chesterton, "The Wild Knight."
5. G. K. Chesterton, "A Glimpse."
6. Chesterton, "The Wild Knight."
7. Augustine, *Confessions* 3.11 (*interior intimo meo*) and 10.38 (*intus eras et ego foris*).

CHAPTER 6

The Perpetual Stream of Prophets

We have always sent messages to people. (28.45)

We have caused Our Word to come to them time after time so that they may be mindful. (28.51)

People who have not read the Qur'an might be surprised at how much of it is devoted to prophets other than Muhammad. Over two dozen men (only men) are called prophets in the book. Each received a revelation from Allah, which he proclaimed by his preaching and his actions. From the time of Adam, these show a record of continual contact with all humankind, from prophet to prophet, along with numerous "messengers," "warners," and "reminders" commissioned by Allah, to keep his people on the right path.

We gave him [*Abraham*] Isaac and Jacob, each of whom We guided, as We had guided Noah before, and among his descendants were David, Solomon, Job, Joseph, Moses, and Aaron—in this way We reward those who do good— Zachariah, John, Jesus, and Elijah—every one of them was righteous—Ishmael, Elisha, Jonah and Lot. We favoured each one of them over other people, and also some of their forefathers, their offspring, and their brothers. We chose them and guided them on a straight path. Such is God's guidance: with it He guides whichever of His servants He will. If they had associated other gods with Him, all their deeds would have come to nothing. Those are the ones to whom We gave the Scripture, wisdom, and prophethood. (6.84–89—cf. 2.135–37)

To ensure an uninterrupted communication of God with his creatures, the Qur'an fills out the list of Old Testament prophets with Arab messengers from the time before Muhammad. They are listed in apparent chronological order as Noah, Hud, Salih, Lot, and Shu'ayb. Hud was sent as a prophet to the people of 'Ad (7.65), Salih to the people of Thamud (7.73), Shu'ayb to the people of Midian (7.85). As Noah and Lot are presumed to have preached in Hebrew, the Arab prophets are probably speaking, like Muhammad, in Arabic. No people can claim not to have heard from their Creator.

Adam

The Qur'an, like both the Jewish and the Christian sacred writings, knows Adam as the first man God created, and the first sinner, who was expelled from his first habitat, the Garden. But the Qur'an also knows Adam in a different way—as the first prophet. After Adam has sinned, repented, and been accepted back by God, he is the first bearer of the Covenant with God, proclaiming that there are no other gods but the one who made him. This makes him the first of God's chosen people, those who carry the message of the One God's care for his believers.

God chose Adam, Noah, Abraham's family, and the family of 'Imran [*father of Mary, the mother of Jesus*], over all other people, in one line of descent—God hears and knows all. (3.33–34)

In Genesis, God forbids Adam and Eve to eat from the tree of the knowledge of good and evil. But Satan convinces Eve that she will be like God if she eats its fruit. Then she gives it to Adam, who was not approached by Satan. Adam eats it to share in Eve's fate. The two, who had not been aware before that they were naked, now feel shame and make coverings for themselves of fig leaves. God, after giving them garments of animal skin, expels them from the Garden, making them mortal (Gn 3.19).

The Qur'an tells a similar but different story. Again, Adam and his spouse are not to eat fruit from a forbidden tree. But Satan does not tempt Eve alone. They are both told that eating the fruit will make them immortal (7.20, 20.120)—which shows that, unlike the biblical Adam and Eve, they were mortal *before* they ate from the tree. But, like the pair in Genesis, they are made aware of their nakedness after eating, and they try to cover themselves with leaves; but God clothes them in what will be the Muslim code of modesty:

We have given you garments to cover your nakedness and as adornment for you; the garment of God-consciousness is the best of all garments—this is one of God's signs, so that people may take heed. (7.26)

The Qur'an version may seem less misogynist than Genesis. A credulous Eve is not the initial target of Satan. Both partners listen to the claim that they will become immortal, and they respond together to Satan's lies. But the Qur'an is definitely patriarchal—as is any seventh-century document. Eve is not Eve in the Qur'an. Women are not important enough to have names—not even Muhammad's wives. Mary the mother of Jesus is the only woman named in the Qur'an—where she cannot simply be "the spouse of So-and-So," since she has no husband. Even her own mother is unnamed—Mary is 'Imran's daughter (66.12). 'Imran's spouse, following the rule, is not named.

Because Adam repents and is forgiven, he passes on to his descendants the truth that there is only One God, preserving the continuity of revelations to mankind. This makes him the original prophet, named twenty-five times in the Qur'an.

Noah

Noah is named even more often than Adam—forty-three times—and he is one of just four who have a surah (71) named for them. Like his namesake in Genesis, he calls on an evil world to repent. In Genesis, every kind of evil in the world is mentioned, where women even mate with Nephilim, supernatural but evil creatures (Gn 6.4). In the Qur'an, by contrast, the great evil is polytheism, since turning away from the One God is the swerve off the "right path" that leads to all other acts of disobedience. In Genesis, God regrets his creation of the world and he decides to kill all humans and even all animals (Gn 6.7). But the virtue of Noah makes God reconsider (Gn 6.8–9), to the extent that he will save Noah and his family. He orders him to build the ark and to bring onto it a male and a female of each species (preventing their extinction) and seven pairs of ritually clean animals (to make continuing sacrifice possible). The book then describes the great flood in detail.

In the Qur'an, by contrast, the flood is just briefly mentioned as the answer to Noah's long prayer asking God to punish a sinful world: "They were drowned and sent to hell" (71.25—equally abrupt at 7.4, 10.73, 21.77). The Qur'an adds some ancillary details not in Genesis—how Noah was mocked while building the ark inland (11.38), how one of his sons refused to board the ark and perished (11.42–43). But the emphasis here, as in the Qur'an's treatment of prophets generally, is on the way they carry the message of God to people, even when the message is rejected.

Abraham

Abraham, the father of nations, is honored by all three "People of the Book" (3.75), Jews and Christians as descendants of a second son, Isaac, and Muslims as descendants of his first son, Ishmael. Abraham's mission and status are mentioned or referred to in 245 verses of the Qur'an. Allah said to him, "I will make you a leader of people" (2.124). And he said:

> Who could be better in religion than those who direct themselves wholly to God, do good, and follow the religion of Abraham, who was true in faith? God took Abraham as a friend. (4.125)

Muslims know Abraham as the rebuilder of the great shrine— the Ka'bah in Mecca, "Your Sacred House" (14.37), the first House to worship the One God (3.96). Muslims face toward it when they pray (2.144), and process around it to culminate their pilgrimage, or hajj (2.125). This site is even more important to Islam than the Temple was to Judaism or the Holy Sepulcher to Christianity. All three places have been the goal of pilgrimages, but no other hajj draws as many devotees as the Ka'bah still does. Tradition holds that the building is on the site of the first sacrifices by Adam and his sons. It was destroyed by the flood in Noah's time, but Abraham is supposed to have rebuilt the present structure from its original foundation stones (2.127).

Later, in Muhammad's time, caravans with different tribesmen placed statues of their local deities in the Ka'bah. When Muhammad tried to restore the Abrahamic place to the One God, he was driven out, to Medina, from which he came back, to conquer the Meccans and purify the building that had been stained with idolatry. Tradition has it (SQ 719) that Muhammad recited this Qur'an verse as he smashed the idols in the Ka'bah:

"The truth has come, and falsehood has passed away: falsehood is bound to pass away." (17.81)

In Genesis, Abraham is commanded explicitly to sacrifice his son Isaac, only to have an angel sent by God prevent this (Gn 22.1–18). In the Qur'an, Abraham has a dream in which he sacrifices his son (37.102–3), which he interprets as an indication of what God wants. His son agrees, and lies down to be killed. God prevents this, praising both father and son for their willingness to make an ultimate sacrifice for God. Instead of substituting a ram for the son, as in Genesis, God says, "We ransomed his son with a momentous sacrifice" (37.107).

The victim in this story, clearly Isaac in Genesis, is unnamed in the Qur'an. Was it Isaac, son of Sarah (Abraham's wife), the second born though of a legal wife, or was it Ishmael, son of Hagar (Sarah's handmaid), the firstborn? Since women are not named in the Qur'an, we cannot identify the sons by their mothers' names. But the sacrifice comes just after Abraham's prayer for progeny has been granted with the promise of a "righteous son" (37.100—SQ has "gentle son"). Since it is later said of Ishmael that "his Lord was well pleased with him" (19.55), there is no stain on him by his birth from a servant. It is only *after* the scene of a son's sacrifice that Isaac's birth is mentioned

(37.112). So what is known in the Jewish and Christian writing as "the sacrifice of Isaac" is in the Qur'an "the sacrifice of Ishmael," and the Muslim line of succession from Abraham is drawn through Ishmael, who had the honor of working with Abraham to rebuild the Ka'bah (2.127).

Moses

> Mention too, in the Scripture, the story of Moses. He was specially chosen, a messenger and a prophet. We called to him from the right-hand side of the mountain and brought him close to Us in secret communion. (19.51–53)

After a string of important but less pivotal prophets, we come to the Big Two: Moses and Jesus. They are given intense treatment in the Qur'an because their followers were the only other monotheists of significant number in areas where Islam took root and spread. The hostile groups there were polytheistic, whose worship of competing gods made up the natural enemy of all three monotheisms. (Atheism was practically nonexistent, and does not figure in the Qur'an.) There were three Covenants for these believers in one God, and each of them was binding on the people to whom it was revealed.

The Jews' Covenant stood out because it was the best organized and the most complete one, an exemplar of the pretemporal or aboriginal Covenant. When "Covenant" is used in the Qur'an without any qualifier, it usually refers to the Jewish Covenant (SQ 1773). That pact with God has a first requirement that is at the very center of Islamic belief:

> I am the Lord your God. . . . You shall have no other god to set against me. . . . You shall not bow down to worship them; for I, the Lord your God, am a jealous god. (Ex 20.1–5)

Though there were partial Covenants with earlier figures, from Adam on, the one revealed to Moses on Mount Sinai deserves special respect. God even tells Muhammad to consult the Torah if he is confused about certain things:

All the messengers We sent before you [*Muhammad*] were simply men to whom We had given the Revelation: you [people] can ask those who have knowledge if you do not know. We sent them with clear signs and scriptures. (16.43–44—cf. 21.7–9)

Moses matters because he is one of a trio of prophets with continuing impact, the other two being Jesus and Muhammad. The mountain of Moses's revelations resembles the cave of Muhammad's revelations. That is why, as we saw earlier, Moses and the mountains proclaim the glory of God.

We made the mountain [*Sinai*] tower high above them at their pledge; We said to them, "Enter the gate" [*to the promised land*] humbly," and, "Do not break the Sabbath," and took a solemn pledge from them. (4.154)

God took [such] a pledge from the Children of Israel. We made twelve leaders [*of the Tribes*] arise among them, and God said, "I am with you: if you keep up prayer, pay the prescribed alms, believe in My messengers and support them, and lend God a good loan, I will wipe out your sins and admit you into Gardens graced with flowing streams." (5.12)

The three faiths should then not argue among themselves (5.68–69, 22.67–68), but should make common cause against their shared opponents, the idolators. Allah wants his believers to be allies, strengthening one another in the various Covenants they have been given:

> We sent Jesus, son of Mary, in their [*the prophets'*] footsteps, to confirm the Torah that had been sent before him: We gave him the Gospel with guidance, light, and confirmation of the Torah already revealed—a guide and lesson for those who take heed of God. . . . We sent to you [Muhammad] the Scripture with the truth, confirming [all] the Scripture that came before and protecting it. (5.46–48)

As the representative of the chosen people dealing directly with God on Mount Sinai, Moses is the most often mentioned or described person in the Qur'an. The general shape of his career is the same as that in the Old Testament—placed as a baby in the Nile, found and taken into Pharaoh's household (28.7–13), killing a man to defend a fellow Israelite (20.40, 28.14–17), exiled to Midian (28.22–28), addressed by a burning fire on Mount Horeb (28.29–35), contending with Pharaoh (20.43–73, 28.36–39), leading people through the Red Sea (7.136–37, 20.77–79), receiving manna (2.57, 7.160), striking a rock to get water (2.60), getting the Tablets on Mount Sinai (7.142–47), destroying the golden calf (7.148–53), putting down the rebellion of Korah (28.76–81).

These events are referred to multiple times, in no particular order. Interesting details are added to the accounts in the Pentateuch. For instance, the manna from heaven is given with an addition of quails. And when Moses strikes the rock, springs break forth from twelve places (spigots as it were), so each of the twelve tribes has its own drinking place. There are some stories told in the Qur'an that have no source in the Bible—as when a perfect sacrifice is ordered to exact specifications by Moses, and then sacrificial parts are made to touch a corpse, which comes temporarily back to life to testify against its murderer (92.67–73).

The glory of Moses is shared by important prophets following him—but none are treated at so great length as Moses. And none has the unique privileges of Jesus.

Jesus

Jesus, unlike all the prophets except Adam, has no human father. Like most of the prophets, but not Muhammad, he works many miracles (3.49). But unlike all the prophets without exception, he is taken up from death directly to God (3.55, 4.158–59). The words used of him set him apart in every way. He is the Word of Allah (3.45), conceived by the inbreathing of the Holy Spirit to Mary (21.91, 66.12), and he will come again at the final judgment (3.55–56). He even repeats Allah's creation of animals from clay (3.49, 5.110). But his preaching is that of all the prophets.

> "I have come to you with a sign from your Lord. Be mindful of God, obey me: God is my Lord and your Lord, so serve Him—that is the straight path." (3.50–51)

Jesus is taught the Torah directly by God:

> "He will teach him the Scripture and wisdom." (3.48)

> We sent Jesus, son of Mary, in their [*earlier prophets'*] footsteps, to confirm the Torah that had been sent before him. We gave him the Gospel with guidance, light, and confirmation of the Torah already revealed—a guide and lesson for those who take heed of God. So let the followers of the

Gospel judge according to what God has set down in it. Those who do not judge according to what God has revealed are lawbreakers. (5.46–47)

With such divine teaching, he is able both to affirm the Torah and yet to remove some things that had been burdensome in it.

"I [*Jesus*] have come to confirm the truth of the Torah which preceded me, and to make some things lawful to you which used to be forbidden." (3.50)

And there is one more distinction marking Jesus out: he is the only prophet who foresees the sending of Muhammad:

"Children of Israel, I am sent to you by God, confirming the Torah that came before me and bringing good news of a messenger to follow me whose name will be Ahmad [*variant of Muhammad*]." (61.6)

The importance of Jesus is prepared for by antecedent miracles, the birth of his forerunner, John, and the unique purity of his mother, Mary. The births of John and Jesus are prepared for by the great piety of their parents. Both Zachariah (John's father) and 'Imran (Mary's father) are priests and prophets, with God's blessing upon them. John is born to an ancient man, Zachariah, and a barren woman (identified only as Zachariah's wife).

This is an account of your Lord's grace towards His servant, Zachariah, when he called to his Lord secretly, saying, "Lord, my bones have weakened and my hair is ashen grey, but never, Lord, have I prayed to You in vain: I fear [what] my kinsmen [will do] when I am gone, for my wife is barren, so grant

me a successor—a gift from You—to be my heir and the heir of
the family of Jacob. Lord, make him well pleasing [to You]."

"Zachariah, We bring you good news of a son whose name
will be John—We have chosen this name for no one before
him." He said, "Lord, how can I have a son when my wife is
barren, and I am old and frail?" He said, "This is what your
Lord has said: 'It is easy for Me: I created you, though you
were nothing before.'" He said, "Give me a sign, Lord." He
said, "Your sign is that you will not speak to anyone for three
full [days and] nights." He went out of the sanctuary to
his people and signalled to them to praise God morning and
evening.

[We said], "John, hold on to the Scripture firmly." While
he was still a boy, We granted him wisdom, tenderness from
Us, and purity. He was devout, kind to his parents, not domineering or rebellious. Peace on him the day he was born, on
the day of his death, and on the day he is raised to life again.
(19.2–15)

Following the artistry of Luke's Gospel, with its parallels
between the births of John and of Jesus, the Qur'an begins its
account of Mary with her father, the prophet and priest 'Imran, and
her unnamed mother (unnamed also in the Gospels but called
Anne in the Christian tradition). 'Imran's wife had dedicated her
unborn child to the priesthood of her husband, but she was surprised (disappointed?) when she gave birth to a little girl. Yet she
kept her resolution to dedicate the girl to God as if the child were
a boy destined for the Temple. This was no ordinary girl.

'Imran's wife said, "Lord, I have dedicated what is growing in
my womb entirely to You; so accept this from me. You are the

One who hears and knows all," but when she gave birth, she said, "My Lord! I have given birth to a girl"—God knew best what she had given birth to: the male is not like the female—"I name her Mary and I commend her and her offspring to Your protection from the rejected Satan." Her Lord graciously accepted her and made her grow in goodness, and entrusted her to the charge of Zachariah. (3.35–37)

Committing the young girl to Zachariah binds the families of John and Jesus even closer than they were said to be in the Gospels. Zachariah realizes that she is being fed by angels (a Mary miracle even before the miraculous virgin birth):

Whenever Zachariah went in to see her in her sanctuary, he found her supplied with provisions. He said, "Mary, how is it you have these provisions?" and she said, "They are from God: God provides limitlessly for whoever He will." (3.37)

When Mary is informed that she will bear Jesus—the Annunciation scene so often painted by great artists—the Qur'an is very close to the Gospel of Luke. In one passage, a delegation of angels has the privilege of carrying the news to her:

The angels said to Mary: "Mary, God has chosen you and made you pure: He has truly chosen you above all women. Mary, be devout to your Lord, prostrate yourself in worship, bow down with those who pray." This is an account of things beyond your knowledge that We reveal to you [Muhammad]: you were not present among them when they cast lots to see which of them should take charge of Mary, you were not present with them when they argued [about her].

The angels said, "Mary, God gives you news of a Word from Him, whose name will be the Messiah, Jesus, son of Mary, who will be held in honour in this world and the next, who will be one of those brought near to God. He will speak to people in his infancy and in his adulthood. He will be one of the righteous." She said, "My Lord, how can I have a son when no man has touched me?" [The angel] said, "This is how God creates what He will: when He has ordained something. He only says, 'Be,' and it is. He will teach him the Scripture and wisdom, the Torah and the Gospel. He will send him as a messenger to the Children of Israel." (3.42–49)

The reference in 3.46—"He will speak to people in his infancy"— is picked up in another account of the Annunciation. In this account, "We sent Our Spirit to appear before her in the form of a normal human" (19.17) to tell her she will bear a son while remaining a virgin. "We shall make him a sign to all people, a blessing from Us" (19.21). But Mary fears that people will not know the miraculous cause of her pregnancy, so she goes into hiding (19.22–26). But then, when the child is born and can no longer be hidden, she is accused of being unchaste, having "done something terrible" (19.27).

She pointed at him. They said, "How can we converse with an infant?" [But] he said, "I am a servant of God. He has granted me the Scripture; made me a prophet; made me blessed wherever I may be. He commanded me to pray, to give alms as long as I live, to cherish my mother. He did not make me domineering or graceless. Peace was on me the day I was born, and will be on me the day I die and the day I am raised to life again." Such was Jesus, son of Mary. (19.29–34)

The unique status of Jesus is proclaimed many times in the Qur'an, even approaching the Pauline view that he is "the second Adam":

We relate to you [Muhammad] this revelation, a decisive statement. In God's eyes Jesus is just like Adam: He created him from dust, said to him "Be," and he was. This is the truth from your Lord, so do not be one of those who doubt. (3.58–60)

Jesus works different miracles:

"I will heal the blind and the leper, and bring the dead back to life with God's permission." (3.49)

One miracle is important enough to merit two accounts of it (3.49 and 5.110):

"I [*Jesus*] will make the shape of a bird for you out of clay, then breathe into it and, with God's permission, it will become a real bird." (3.49)

The second account repeats that it is Allah's power that is working through Jesus:

"By My leave, you fashioned the shape of a bird out of clay, breathed into it, and it became, by My leave, a bird." (5.110)

This is as close as a human being can come to repeating the miracle by which Adam was created out of dust—down to the inbreathing by which God animates his creatures.

The importance of Jesus in God's plans for all of history is appreciated by Maria Massi Dakake:

The uniqueness of Jesus among the messengers is affirmed in several ways, including his title *Ruh Allah* ("Spirit of God"). He is referred to here and in certain places, however, as the *Messiah* (*al-Masih*), a term that in Arabic is understood to refer to his having been purified by God of sin. This is not unrelated to the concept of being "anointed," the root meaning of the word in Hebrew. He is also identified as God's *Word*, an idea that has clear resonance with the Gospel tradition, where Jesus is identified as the "Word" of God (see Jn 1). . . . In the Islamic context, the identification of Jesus as God's *Word* does not preclude or overshadow his function as the bringer of the Gospel, which, like the Torah and the Quran, represents God's Word and message to humanity. . . . However, while all created beings are brought into existence through God's Word, Christ alone is specifically identified as "a Word from God." Some might argue, therefore, that Jesus, by virtue of being identified as God's Word, somehow participates (uniquely) in the Divine Creative Command, although this is not the traditional Islamic understanding of Jesus' identification as a Word from Him. (SQ 267)

While Dakake is right to stress that Jesus can never be divine in the monotheistic values of the Qur'an, and those who worship him as such are departing from the authentic revelation, no one comes closer to being *all but* divine. His importance in the Islamic scheme of salvation history is clear. Jesus will be vindicated on the Last Day:

God said, "Jesus, I will take you back and raise you up to Me: I will purify you of the disbelievers. To the Day of

Resurrection I will make those who followed you superior to those who disbelieved. Then you will all return to Me and I will judge between you regarding your differences. I will make the disbelievers suffer severely in this world and the next; no one will help them." As for those who believe and do good deeds God will pay them their reward in full but God does not love evildoers. (3.55–57)

Some Jews denied Mary's virginity and tried to kill Jesus as a way of proving he was not the Messiah. But God thwarted their plot.

God has sealed them in their disbelief, so they believe only a little—and because they disbelieved and uttered a terrible slander against Mary, and said, "We have killed the Messiah, Jesus, son of Mary, the Messenger of God." (They did not kill him, nor did they crucify him, though it was made to appear like that to them; those that disagreed about him are full of doubt, with no knowledge to follow, only supposition: they certainly did not kill him—No! God raised him up to Himself. God is almighty and wise. There is not one of the People of the Book who will not believe in [Jesus] before his death, and on the Day of Resurrection he will be a witness against them.) (4.155–59)[1]

Jesus is a messenger for all believers, just as Moses and Muhammad are.

The Continuity of Revelation

It is clear that Muhammad's revelations were meant to lay a basis for peaceful relations between followers of Torah, Gospel, and Qur'an. Any Muslim developments that deny or cancel these foundations are Islamic heresies. Muslim orthodoxy lies in the Qur'an, with its celebration of Moses and Jesus as great prophets of the One God. Allah tells believers to speak this way:

"We believe in God and in what was sent down to us and what was sent down to Abraham, Ishmael, Isaac, Jacob, and the Tribes, and what was given to Moses, Jesus, and all the prophets by their Lord. We make no distinction between any of them, and we devote ourselves to Him."

Say [Prophet] [to the Jews and Christians], "How can you argue with us about God when He is our Lord and your Lord? Our deeds belong to us, and yours to you. We devote ourselves entirely to Him." (2.136, 139)

The followers of all God's prophets are natural brothers, not enemies. Thus, when the Qur'an permits defensive war against aggressors, it does so for all the places where the One God is worshipped.

If God did not repel some people by means of others, many monasteries, churches, synagogues, and mosques, where God's name is much invoked, would have been destroyed. (22.40)

Allah protects equally the synagogue, the church, and the mosque—the people of Moses, of Jesus, and of Muhammad.

NOTES

1. The words "before his death" can refer, says Dakake, to his "seeming death" mentioned in 4.17 or to the way God takes Jesus up from life, keeping him for the final day, when he will die and be resurrected with the rest of humankind:

Islamic tradition holds Jesus will return near the end times to fight the Antichrist (al-Dajjal) and will thereafter eventually die and be resurrected with the rest of humanity. (SQ 263)

Dakake interprets in the same way the verses where the infant Jesus speaks, saying:

> Peace was on me the day I was born, and will be on me the day I die and the day I am raised to life again. (19.33)

Of this she writes:

> He will be free from fear on the day he dies (after his return to earth: see 43.61, commentary) and on the day he is raised alive with the rest of humanity (see commentary on 4.157-59). (SQ 773)

CHAPTER 7

Peace to Believers

Say, "People of the Book, you have no true basis [for your religion] unless you uphold the Torah, the Gospel, and that which has been sent down to you [*Muhammad*] from your Lord." (5.68)

"We make no distinction between any of His messengers." (2.285)

Enough was said in the last chapter about Allah as the author equally of the Torah, the Gospel, and the Qur'an. But what if one revelation conflicts with another? May one appeal to a revelation given to another people? Allah seems to say no:

We have assigned a law and a path to each of you. If God had so willed, He would have made you one community, but He wanted to test you through that which He has given you, so race to do good: you will all return to God and He will make clear to you the matters you differed about. So [Prophet] judge between them according to what God has sent down [*to them*]. Do not follow their whims, and take good care that they do not tempt you away from any of what God has sent down to you. (5.48–49)

It is clear that God wants each body of believers to live by the Covenant given it. Each was, as it were, tailored to its particular assignment for "testing" the relationship with God. To look for another Covenant is to slip back into a form of polytheism, as if a different God, not the same one, could be in a different revelation. There should not be appeal *away from* one revelation to another but "good works" affirming their amity.

All three "People of the Book" are criticized when they depart from the message sent especially to them. This should not be surprising. The fact that God gives a revelation to a people does not mean that they will always be observant of it. God's patience and mercy show in the fact that human beings constantly fail to keep their commitment to the Covenant, which has to be constantly renewed, under the spur and the consolation of the prophets. Mercy is God's leading trait, and it is called on at every stage of what might be called the covenantal cycle—moving from adherence, through failure, to renewal. As Joseph Lumbard puts it in *The Study Quran:*

The Quran presents itself as part of the unbroken chain of Abrahamic scriptures in which God renews the covenant, only to have it broken by human beings and forgotten time and again. Then, through mercy and love, He relents unto humanity, providing another reminder of the eternal covenant and a new means for observing it. The Quranic covenant is thus a continuation of sacred history presented as both a

reaffirmation of the one pretemporal covenant and an extension of the covenant(s) that God made through the Torah and
the Gospels. (SQ 1781)

There are many cases of God's people trying to escape the
commitments of their own Covenant. Sometimes they do this by
appealing to one of the other revelations, one not meant specially for
them. They attempt to escape the terms of God's particular message
for them. That occurs in all of the three main revelations.

Muslims Flee the Qur'an

Looking to other revelations for protection was a temptation that
could come naturally to Muslims—they were, after all, history's
new kids on the block when Muhammad was delivering the Qur'an
to them. People of the Torah and the Gospel had been around for
a longer time in history. They had forged some grounds for coexis-
tence with the pagans who seemed so powerful in seventh-century
Arabia. That is the situation behind this passage:

> You who believe, do not take the Jews and Christians as
> allies: they are allies only to each other. Anyone who takes
> them as an ally becomes one of them—God does not guide
> such wrongdoers—yet you [Prophet] will see the perverse at
> heart rushing to them for protection, saying, "We are afraid
> fortune may turn against us." (5.51–52)

To say that Muhammad's followers cannot be allies of the other
People of the Book is not to reject other revelations. The Qur'an is
saying that Muslims cannot run under the shield of another people
for protection, as if the Qur'an were not a strong enough pledge on

God's part to protect his people. That would be a way of pitting church or synagogue against mosque under the pretense of forming an "alliance."

There are other ways that Muslims disobey their Covenant, and Allah has to comfort Muhammad when he despairs of getting his message through to them; but this, as Lumbard says, is the ordinary struggle with those a prophet has to take the message to.

Jews Flee the Torah

We have seen that Jesus reaffirms the Torah but also removes some of its more burdensome demands. He says:

> "I have come to confirm the truth of the Torah which preceded me, and to make some things lawful to you which used to be forbidden." (3.50)

Does one prophet have the right to change another prophet's revelation? That seems to go against the command to live within your particular Covenant. Some explain that Jesus, having been taught the Torah directly by God, is just affirming changes Allah had already made for the Jews—first imposing restrictions as punishment, then removing them:

> For the wrongdoings done by the Jews, We forbade them certain good things that had been permitted to them before: for having frequently debarred others from God's path; for taking usury when they had been forbidden to do so; and for wrongfully devouring other people's property. For those of them that reject the truth We have prepared an agonizing torment. But those of them who are well grounded in knowledge

and have faith do believe in what has been revealed to you [Muhammad], and in what was revealed before you—those who perform the prayers, pay the prescribed alms, and believe in God and the Last Day—to them We shall give a great reward. (4.160–62)

This has been used to show that the Qur'an is anti-Semitic (though not nearly as anti-Semitic as the New Testament Gospel of John or Letter to the Hebrews). And it should be remembered that the Old Testament itself often rebukes God's people for ignoring the Covenant, killing the prophets (Jer 2.30, 26.20–23), and treating the poor unjustly. Usury was forbidden in Jewish law (Ex 22.25, Lv 25.36–37), yet some Jews fell back on the practice (4.161).

It has been suggested that the conflicts over Jewish laws largely pertained to dietary restrictions.[1] But the real issue between Muslims and Jews seems to have been over disparity of punishments for things like adultery. Jewish adulterers, for instance, could appeal from stoning under the Torah (Dt 22.22–24) to flogging under the Qur'an:

Strike the adulteress and the adulterer one hundred times. Do not let compassion for them keep you from carrying out God's law. (24.2)

Harsh as both punishments are, a person can live after the flogging but not after the stoning. But in any case the Qur'an forbids such "judge shopping."

Why do they [Jews] come to you [Muslims] for judgement when they have the Torah with God's judgement, and even then still turn away? These are not [Jewish] believers. We revealed the Torah with guidance and light, and the prophets, who had submitted to God, judged according to it for the Jews. So did the rabbis and the scholars in accordance with that part of God's Scripture which they were entrusted to preserve, and to which they were witnesses. (5.43–44)

Maria Massi Dakake writes of this passage:

[It] indicates that the Torah and the Gospel remain valid sources of moral and legal judgment and guidance for Jews and Christians, respectively, even after the coming of the Prophet—indeed, even in his presence. . . . [These passages] enjoin the Jewish Authorities and scholars to preserve the Torah as it had been revealed and to avoid altering it, either out of fear of others or to gain wealth and social standing by changing the laws to suit influential people. (SQ 298)

The situation is complicated if it envisages an area where Muslims rule and Jews and Christians are left to observe their religion so long as they pay taxes to maintain government services. There may be instances where a judgment is expected of the Muslim authorities in their peacekeeping role. Allah tells them to avoid this if possible, but to rule, if they must, justly:

If they come to you [Prophet] for judgement, you can either judge between them or decline—if you decline, they will not harm you in any way, but if you do judge between them, judge justly: God loves the just. (5.42)

Some take this to mean the Prophet should judge by the Qur'an (which was still in process of being revealed to the Prophet), but a more natural sense is given by Dakake, that "he should judge the People of the Book according to what God has sent down to them,

namely, their own scriptures" (SQ 300). The different congregations
have trouble observing the demands of their own Covenant, and
should not get distracted by calculation of what they could do under
other dispensations.

Jane Dammen McAuliffe has written that "whatever praise is
cautiously meted out to Christians [in the Qur'an] is produced with
a concomitant denigration of the Jews."[2] It is true that Muhammad's new foundation in Medina came into more conflict with
Jewish inhabitants there than with Christians. This does not mean
that the Torah is rated lower than the Gospel. The only criticism of
the Jews is for not observing their own Torah—for doubting Moses,
for trying to kill Jesus, and for taking usury (4.153–61)—but the
book instantly promises Jews who do observe the Torah that their
place in heaven is assured (4.162). Those who do not follow the
Torah are as incapable of getting its rewards as if they were animals
unable to read it.

> Those who have been charged to obey the Torah, but do not
> do so, are like asses carrying books. (62.5)

Christians Fleeing the Gospel

It is true that there are fewer criticisms of Christians in the Qur'an
than of Jews, but the censured faults are deeper and more momentous than any derelictions from the Torah. Christians have one great
sin, which has caused factionalism between sects of those who stay
true to the Gospel, in which Jesus is a prophet of the One God, and
those who revert to polytheism, saying Jesus is one of three gods,
who form a partnership like the partnerships of gods adored by
pagans. No prophet is praised in the Qur'an more than Jesus. But
that means his followers take a more horrible fall when they give
up their Covenant with the One God. There is nothing explicit in

the Gospel that says Jesus is divine, or that he is part of a trinity of the divine being. That doctrine would be worked out, amid much controversy, by the fourth century, at the Council of Nicaea. The Qur'an sees this development as a sin of sins.

Modern anthropologists generally suppose there is an original religiosity that finds different gods in different powers of nature, and that it gets refined into a powerful God of gods whose nature is expanded into monotheism. The Qur'an, by contrast, affirms that a knowledge of the One God was instilled into Adam and all his descendants. From this orthodoxy they fall off into the worship of idols, like Moses's followers deserting Yahweh for the golden calf. Christians are the most egregious offenders in this respect, in that they are the most successful.

> Those people who say that God is the third of three are defying [the truth]: there is only One God. . . . The Messiah, son of Mary, was only a messenger. (5.73, 75)

> People of the Book, do not go to excess in your religion, and do not say anything about God except the truth: the Messiah, Jesus, son of Mary, was nothing more than a messenger of God, His word directed to Mary, and a spirit from Him. So believe in God and his messengers and do not say "three." (4.171)

> When God says, "Jesus, son of Mary, did you say to people, 'Take me and my mother as two gods alongside God'?" he will say, "May You be exalted! I would never say what I had no right to say—if I had said any such thing You would have known it: You know all that is within me, though I do not know what is within You, You alone have full knowledge of things unseen—I told them only what You commanded me

to: 'Worship God, my Lord and your Lord.' I was a witness over them during my time among them. Ever since You took my soul, You alone have been the watcher over them: You are witness to all things and if You punish them, they are Your servants; if You forgive them, You are the Almighty, the Wise." (5.116–18)

The Qur'an's teaching is not far from that of Christians who believe in a "primitive Christianity" before the Council of Nicaea in the fourth century. Even after that council, various "Arianizing" movements believed what Unitarians do today—that Jesus was the highest and greatest of human beings, without being God. Humanists like Thomas Jefferson have held similar views. Is the Qur'an therefore "anti-Christian"? It is more anti-Nicaean. It holds that Trinitarian "Christians" are not Gospel Christians. This has not prevented Pope Francis from praying to the One God with his beloved Muslims (*The Joy of the Gospel* par. 254). This ecumenical approach is responded to from the Muslim side by Maria Massi Dakake in *The Study Quran:*

> The [Quran] criticism [of the Trinity] seems directed at those who assert the existence of three distinct "gods," an idea that Christians themselves reject. . . . Despite these strong criticisms of Christian trinitarian doctrine as well as the implication through juxtaposition in 5.72–73 that Christian beliefs in the divinity of Jesus, and in God as *the third of three* can be understood as a kind of *shirk* (ascribing partners unto God), Islamic Law never considered Christians to be "idolaters" (*mushrikun*) and accepted Christians' own assertions of monotheistic belief, maintaining the clear distinction the Quran itself makes between idolaters (*mushrikun*) and the People of the Book. (SQ 267–68)

Dakake's may be a minority view among Islamists at this moment. The future of ecumenical relations between Muslims and Christians may depend on Pope Francis's claim not only that Unitarians and humanists are right about Jesus, but that Trinitarianism should be so defined as to be a monotheistic belief—as Augustine taught.

Are Torah and Gospel "Abrogated" by Qur'an?

Despite all that is said in the Qur'an about the divine authorship of Torah and Gospel and Qur'an, some think that the last of these cancels out the other two; they think this is the meaning of *naskh* (abrogation) in passages like this:

> Any revelation We cause to be superseded or forgotten, We replace with something better or similar. Do you [Prophet] not know that God has power over everything? (2.106)

We have seen that God changed dietary laws for the Jews as punishment; but does this intra-testamental power extend to inter-testamental powers? And can it refer not to details of a religion but to a cancellation of an entire Covenant, rescinding the entire Torah and/or the entire Gospel? That seems impossible after God's praise of each body of revelation as reflecting his care for all his people. God tells Muhammad to follow what he is telling him and let other believers observe their own set of revelations:

> We have sent down the Qur'an to give judgement in the Arabic language. . . . We sent messengers before you [*Muhammad*]. . . . There was a Scripture for every age: God erases or confirms whatever He will, and the source of Scripture is with Him. Whether We let you [Prophet] see part of what We threaten

them [*other People of the Book*] with, or cause you to die [before that], your duty is only to deliver the message: the Reckoning is Ours. (13.37–40)

Allah declares that he has changed what he was teaching Muhammad "step by step," and that others have doubted the whole teaching because of inconsistencies; but they must learn to trust the teaching process:

> When We substitute one revelation for another—and God knows best what He reveals—they say, "You [*Prophet*] are just making it up," but most of them have no knowledge. Say that the Holy Spirit has brought the Revelation with the Truth step by step from your Lord, to strengthen the believers and as guidance and good news to the devout. (16.101–2)

This "substitution" of one revelation for another is taking place within the revelation to Muhammad as he deals with unbelievers. These unbelievers are being answered in another passage:

> [Prophet], they ask you about the Spirit. Say, "The Spirit is part of my Lord's domains. You have only been given a little knowledge." If We pleased, We could take away what We have revealed to you—then you would find no one to plead for you against Us—if it were not for your Lord's mercy. (17.85–87)

Here, as often, God is trying to cheer up Muhammad in his difficulties. He says that the revelations present obstacles to the weak in faith, but things could be worse—God could take the Qur'an away from dispute, but then Muhammad would have nothing to vindicate him.

The idea that abrogation applies only to verses within the Qur'an comports with the language used of Torah and Gospel throughout the Qur'an. To quote Joseph Lumbard again: "The Quran never declares that the Covenant as observed by previous religious communities has been abrogated or rendered obsolete" (SQ 1774).[3] Gibbon, in his fair summary of Muslim beliefs, wrote: "The liberality of Mahomet allowed to his predecessors the same credit which he claimed for himself; and the chain of inspiration was prolonged from the fall of Adam to the promulgation of the Koran."[4]

Islamists accept the principle that naskh is applicable only within the Qur'an; it does not obliterate whole other revelations. This is so true that Muhammad, if he is uncertain about God's word, can clarify it by checking what he has revealed to others:

> [Prophet], all the messengers We sent before you were simply men to whom We had given the Revelation: you [people] can ask those who have knowledge if you do not know. We sent them with clear signs and scriptures. We have sent down the message to you too [Prophet], so that you can explain to people what was sent for them, so that they may reflect. (16.43–44)

Commenting on 16.43, Dakake observes that "those who know" about other revelations may be Jews or Christians or Muslims who are knowledgeable about Torah and Gospel (SQ 667).

Those who recognize that abrogation is meant to be intratestamental still find it hard to tell which verses are abrogated by other verses. One would expect later ones to revise earlier ones, but the chronology for many of them is hard to establish. Also, moral precepts are more often stated generally than specifically. That is why respected scholars identify a wide range of naskhs—as few as 5, as many as 250 (SQ 49). Islam recognized a problem that all believers in a divine revelation have to deal with—namely, if there are contrary statements in the sacred writings, how can they all be attributed to God? Some Jews cope with this by distinctions in the Halakha, some Protestants by "dispensationalism," some Catholics by what Newman called "the development of doctrine." Naskh is the Muslim equivalent of those thought processes.

One of the more obvious naskhs is the surah that forbids alcohol, over against the several verses that (partly) allow it (SQ 322, 685):

You who believe, intoxicants and gambling, idolatrous practices, and [divining with] arrows are repugnant acts—Satan's doing—shun them so that you may prosper. (5.90)[5]

Even this blanket prohibition is more related to dietary laws than to the great moral issues. The last word on the threefold revelation granted to all God's prophets seems to be given in Surah 41, where the seal of prophecy is not to supersede what came before but to confirm it:

[Remember that] you [Prophet] are not told anything that the previous messengers were not told. (41.43)

Apostates

If the Qur'an is fraternal in its treatment of other faiths, why is it so ferocious to "hypocrites" and apostates in the religion of Allah? Certain parallels exist in the Jewish and Christian communities. Embattled monotheists, in a culture still infested by polytheists, need to maintain solidarity in their most important and distinctive characteristic—the belief in one and only one God. Any backsliding here is a desertion of the cause at its very core—whether it is worshipping a gold calf or throwing incense on a Roman sacrificial object.

Since the main moral issue in the Qur'an is maintenance of belief in the One God against persecution from the polytheists, martyrs to the truth are the heroes of the book, and those who just feign belief in the One God (hypocrites) and those who abandon it, either from fear of persecution or in plain error, are history's villains. The One God is a jealous God:

> God does not forgive the worship of others beside Him— though He does forgive whoever He will for lesser sins—for whoever does this has gone far, far astray. In His place the idolaters invoke only females, and Satan, the rebel God rejected. (4.116–17)

The mention of female gods refers to the three Arabian tribal goddesses honored as God's divine daughters in the Ka'bah before Muhammad purified it:

> [Disbelievers], consider al-Lat and al-'Uzza, and the third, other one, Manat—are you to have the male and He the female [*daughter goddesses*]? That would be a most unjust distribution!—these are nothing but names you have invented yourselves, you and your forefathers. God has sent no authority for them. These people merely follow guesswork and the whims of their souls, even though guidance has come to them from their Lord. (53.19–23)[6]

The early days of Islam and of Christianity placed a high regard on maintaining fidelity to the group against the threat of persecution. Those who gave in to threats and abandoned the faith were traitors, were turncoats. Those who defied death and became martyrs were the rock stars of both infant movements.

Candida Moss is right to say that the persecution of early Christians was exaggerated—sporadic crackdowns were never a continuous reign of terror.[7] But the perceived threat was a great unifier of the embattled core of believers, who could have frayed out from initial uncertainties in a community still defining itself. There was little mercy to those "traitors" who turned over scripture to be destroyed or threw incense on a sacrificial victim. Those Christians who did this lost their consecration as bishops or ordination as priests, and some had to be rebaptized to be admitted into the church again—if they could rejoin even then.

Christians who fell could not easily be readmitted. If they fell again, they were forever excluded. As Ambrose of Milan put it, "As there is only one baptism, there is only one penance."[8] The hard line on apostates was expressed in the Letter to the Hebrews misattributed to Saint Paul:

> If we sin again on purpose, after seeing the truth, no sacrifice remains for our sins, only a terrifying judgment to come, and a wild fire voracious of recalcitrants. Anyone rejecting the Law of Moses dies without pity if two or three testify. What worse punishment will he earn who has trampled on the Son of God, disdaining the blood of the Pact in which he was cleansed, and mocking the favors of the Spirit? We know, of course, who says, "Punishment is mine, I shall exact it," and "The Lord will judge his people." Fearful it is to fall into the hands of the living God. (Heb 10.26–31)

The Qur'an is not as absolute as this, because it always leaves room for God's inexhaustible mercy and forgiveness.

The Family of Believers

> Say, "People of the Book, let us arrive at a statement that is common to us all: we worship God alone, we ascribe no partner to Him, and none of us takes others beside God as lords." (3.64)

The solidarity of believers in the One God is reflected in the Qur'an's marriage laws. Muslims may marry Jews or Christians without compromising the religion of any of the parties. In fact, Muhammad gave sanction to this by marrying a Jew (Safiyya bint Huyayy) and taking a Coptic Christian as a concubine (Marya al-Qibtiyya).[9]

> Today all good things have been made lawful for you. The food of the People of the Book is lawful for you as your food is lawful for them. So are chaste, believing, women as well as chaste women of the people who were given the Scripture before you, as long as you have given them their bride-gifts and married them, not taken them as lovers or secret mistresses. (5.5)

The mention of chaste women does not solely mean virgins. The Qur'an's constant references to penitence and forgiveness mean, according to Maria Massi Dakake in *The Study Quran*, that forgiveness can repristinate the sinner.

> *Chaste women* translates *muhsanat,* which may mean either "chaste women" or "free women," and the term has been interpreted differently in this context. When it is interpreted to mean "chaste," it is understood to refer to the woman's present status, not necessarily to her past actions, for women who had been unchaste but then repented regained their "chaste" status and were eligible for marriage. (SQ 277)

This celebration of "all good things made lawful" indicates how Muslims and Jews and Christians should treat each other. As Dakake notes,

This verse allows intermarriage with the People of the Book, suggesting the possibility of extensive social relations between Muslims and members of these religious communities. (SQ 277)

Those who would introduce discord into the relations of the believers are at odds with Qur'an-observing Muslims.

NOTES

1. For instance in this passage:

   We forbade for the Jews every animal with claws [*carnivores*], and the fat of cattle and sheep, except what is on their backs and in their intestines, or that which sticks to their bones. This is how We penalized them for their disobedience. (6.146)

2. Jane Dammen McAuliffe, *Qur'anic Christians: An Analysis of Classical and Modern Exegesis* (Cambridge University Press, 1991), p. 159.

3. See also Caner K. Dagli on 3.85 (SQ 153–54). Some Islamic scholars, outside the mainstream, do not admit that naskh applies even to the Qur'an. See Osman Tastan, "Huseyin Atay's Approach to Understanding the Qur'an," in Suha Taji-Farouki ed., *Modern Muslim Intellectuals and the Qur'an* (Oxford University Press, 2004), pp. 241–62.

4. Edward Gibbon, *The History of the Decline and Fall of the Roman Empire*, ed. David Womersley (Penguin, 1994), vol. 3, p. 178.

5. The other passages are less absolute:

   From the fruits of date palms and grapes you take sweet [*fermented*] juice and wholesome provisions. (16.67)

   You who believe, do not come anywhere near the prayer if you are intoxicated, not until you know what you are saying. (4.43)

   They ask you [Prophet] about intoxicants and gambling: say, "There is great sin in both, and some benefit for people: the sin is greater than the benefit." (2.219)

6. The three prominent goddesses had their own separate shrines in Arabia, but they would have been honored by their respective tribal worshippers when they came to the holy city of Mecca. The myth of the "Satanic Verses" used

in Salman Rushdie's novel came from praise of these three goddesses that Satan supposedly whispered to Muhammad after they were named at 53.19, calling them "high flying cranes" whose intercession would be powerful (SQ 1292–93).

7. Candida Moss, *The Myth of Persecution: How Early Christians Invented a Story of Martyrdom* (HarperOne, 2013). Moss was building on insights earlier expressed by Geoffrey de Ste. Croix, "Why Were the Early Christians Persecuted?," in M. I. Finley, *Studies in Ancient Society* (Routledge and Kegan Paul, 1974), and Glenn Bowersock, *Martyrdom and Rome* (Cambridge University Press, 1998).

8. Ambrose, *De Paenitentia* 2.10.

9. Jonathan A. C. Brown, *Muhammad: A Very Short Introduction* (Oxford University Press, 2011), pp. 49, 51.

CHAPTER 8

Zeal (Jihad)

For the zeal of thine house hath eaten me up.

—PS 69.9 (KJV)

"Jihad" has a range of meanings, as does its English equivalent, "zeal." This, like jihad, means "striving." One can strive for excellence or strive to destroy something. To describe a person as having zeal can be a matter for praise or blame. But "zealous" edges toward extremism, and "zealot" reaches that unacceptable fringe. It means "fanatic." Still, it would be a mistake to brand all kinds of zeal as fanatical.

The same is true of "crusade." We often think of that as a campaign for something good, a striving toward it. Dwight Eisenhower called his 1948 war memoir *Crusade in Europe*. Billy Graham called his revivals crusades. The influential evangelical movement founded by Bill Bright in 1951 was called Campus Crusade for Christ. That did not mean the evangelizers were at war with any university that hosted a chapter of their movement. But the term had become tainted enough by 2011 for the name to be changed, from Campus Crusade for Christ to Cru.

Some on the religious right called this a "politically correct" effort to get rid of the name Christ. Actually, it was a recognition that crusade is no longer an unequivocally good thing. It was prompted, in part, by the backlash against George W. Bush's blunder when he said on the South Lawn of the White House, a week after 9/11, "This crusade, this war on terrorism, is going to take a while." For him, the word still had Billy Graham associations. He meant to be preaching a crusade for democracy, as Graham preached a crusade for Christ. He also said on the South Lawn that terrorists attack us because "they can't stand freedom." But there was a shudder throughout the Middle East over his used of the hated term "crusade."

I became aware of the toxicity of that word in the Middle East during my first visit to Israel many years ago. I had read T. E. Lawrence's Oxford thesis on Crusader castles, and I expressed an interest in looking at structures he had especially praised. I was soon told that "crusader" was a time-bomb word. And if that is true even of Israelis, how much more explosive is it for Muslims? For them, it is a sign of the Christian West's age-old aggressions against that whole part of the world.

The American view of crusades was heavily influenced by Cecil B. DeMille's 1935 movie, *The Crusades,* where Henry Wilcoxon as Richard I ("Lionheart") woos Loretta Young as the princess Berengaria and wins back Jerusalem for the Christians. Richard I is also glorified in Michael Curtiz's 1938 movie *The Adventures of Robin Hood,* where Errol Flynn as Robin woos Olivia de Havilland as Maid Marian before helping "Lionheart" reclaim his England. Those movies were the model for dozens of imitations and they gave the word "crusade" a rosy glow in Western minds, while it is stained a dirty blood-red in the Arabic world.

That shows how the same word can be revered by some groups and reviled by others. That is true, now, of "jihad." For one culture it means a striving for moral discipline and observance of the Qur'an, sometimes (but not always) while waging a just war. In another culture, it always means "holy war," though there is no word for that in the Qur'an (SQ 1805).[1] Allah tells Muhammad to wage jihad against unbelievers "with this Qur'an" (25.52), which means by the arguments for monotheism. The Qur'an never advocates war as a means of religious conversion, since "there is no compulsion in religion" (2.256). In fact, Muhammad lived for the first ten years of his revelations at peace with the surrounding polytheists of Mecca.[2]

Just (Defensive) War

It was only when he was driven out of Mecca by his own tribe, the Quraysh, who then besieged his followers in Medina, that Allah gave Muhammad justifications for defensive war.

> Those who have been attacked are permitted to take up arms because they have been wronged—God has the power to help them—those who have been driven unjustly from their homes only for saying, "Our Lord is God." (22.39–40)

This permission aligns Muslims with other monotheists fighting for their "monasteries, churches, synagogues, and mosques" (22.40).

This kind of war must be waged, as all good works are in the Qur'an, *fi sabil illah*, "in the way of God." That means that even defensive war must observe moral limits, including a scale proportioned to the attack, not going beyond what is necessary to overcome the attackers.

Fight in God's cause against those who fight you, but do not
overstep the limits: God does not love those who overstep the
limits. (2.190)

The existence of the Ka'bah in Mecca gave a special inhibition
against war in its sacred area. Caravans of warring tribes disarmed
to observe a peace code. But this exposed them to attack by people
willing to break the code. Therefore Allah says that if one is attacked
on sacred ground, one can respond even in the vicinity of the Ka'bah:

Do not fight them at the Sacred Mosque unless they fight
you there. If they do fight you, kill them—this is what such disbelievers deserve—but if they stop, then God is most forgiving
and merciful. Fight them until there is no more persecution,
and worship [*at the shrine*] is devoted to God. If they cease
hostilities, there can be no [further] hostility, except towards
aggressors. A sacred month for a sacred month [*of devotion at
the shrine, but*]: violation of sanctity [calls for] fair retribution.
So if anyone commits aggression against you, attack him as [*in
proportion with how*] he attacked you, but be mindful of God,
and know that He is with those who are mindful of Him.
(2.191–94)

The sentence immediately preceding this passage is often
quoted on its own as a kind of license to kill anywhere, when it is
clear from context what is being said:

Kill them wherever you encounter them [*that is, even in the
sacred area*], and drive them out from where they drove you
out, for persecution [*on religious grounds*] is more serious than
killing [*in self-defense*]. (2.191)

This is a criticism of holy war (persecution), not a defense of it. Indeed, "holy war," sometimes taken as a definition of jihad, is not a concept expressed anywhere in the Qur'an.

Since the first wars of Muhammad took him from the besieged Medina back to the launching area of his enemies, Mecca with its shrine, all the talk about war's morality is concentrated on the justification of war in and around the Ka'bah. The Quraysh tribe cannot be given impunity for its aggression against Muslims because of having an un-invadable base for its operations. Consciousness of and scruples about the special circumstances of this kind of war become clear from the passage I just quoted. Muhammad Abdel Haleem writes about it:

> In six verses (2.190–95) we find four prohibitions ("do not"), six restrictions: two "until," two "if," two "who attack you," as well as such cautions as "in the way of God," "be conscious of God," "God does not like those who overstep the limits," "God is with those who are conscious of Him," "with those who do good deeds" and "God is Forgiving, Merciful." It should be noted that the Qur'an, in treating the theme of war, as with many other themes, regularly gives the reasons and justifications for any action it demands.[3]

The pacific attitude toward outsiders applied as well to internal conflicts among Muslims, where Allah tells his followers to side with the group suffering aggression (oppression):

> If two groups of the believers fight, you [believers] should try to reconcile them; if one of them oppresses the other, fight the oppressors until they submit to God's command, then make a just and even-handed reconciliation between the two of them: God loves those who are even-handed. The believers

are brothers, so make peace between your two brothers and
be mindful of God, so that you may be given mercy. (49.9–10)

But not all divisions can be settled by persuasive or coercive
intervention. If people persist in their evil ways, they should be left
alone (so long as they are not actively committing aggression on the
innocent), and God will sort things out at the final judgment:

> If anyone opposes the Messenger, after guidance has been
> made clear to him, and follows a path other than that of the
> believers, We [*Allah*] shall leave him on his chosen path—
> We shall burn him in Hell, an evil destination. (4.115)

That one should abstain from violence to the degree that that
is possible is apparent from the Qur'an's treatment (5.27–32) of
what we know as the Cain and Abel story from Genesis (Gn 4.1–8).
In both places, the teaching is against spiritual envy (over the success or failure of a sacrificial rite) and against murder. But the Abel
figure (the "sons of Adam" are not given names in the Qur'an) is
more principled in opposition to violence:

> One said, "I will kill you," but the other said, "God only
> accepts the sacrifice of those who are mindful of Him. If you
> raise your hand to kill me, I will not raise mine to kill you. I
> fear God, the Lord of all worlds, and I would rather you were
> burdened with my sins as well as yours and became an inhab-
> itant of the Fire: such is the evildoers' reward." But his soul
> prompted him to kill his brother: he killed him and became
> one of the losers. (5.27–30)

This differs from the Genesis account in three important points.
(1) The Abel figure will not answer violence with violence. How

does this comport with the fact that God permits defensive war? One explanation is that one of the two heirs of Adam does not want to kill half the human progeny. There are as yet no others this figure would be defending—no spouse or children or church fellows or patria—and one cannot preempt the first murder (there is no retribution until after it occurs). This is a way of emphasizing (2) the deepest meaning of murder:

> We decreed to the Children of Israel that if anyone kills a person—unless in retribution for murder or spreading corruption in the land—it is as if he kills all mankind, while if any saves a life it is as if he saves the lives of all mankind. (5.32)

Finally, (3) the possibility of mercy, as in the case of Adam and his spouse, is always there. "He became remorseful" (5.31) and God showed him, by a raven's example, how to avoid the ritual disgrace of leaving the body exposed. The lesson throughout is to show a reverence for God's creatures, and to repent and make what amends you can if you fail.

A "Sword Verse"?

The wrenching of words from their context is most obvious in letting the so-called sword verse stand alone:

> When the [four] forbidden months are over, wherever you encounter the idolaters, kill them, seize them, besiege them, wait for them at every lookout post; but if they repent, maintain the prayer, and pay the prescribed alms, let them go on their way, for God is most forgiving and merciful. (9.5)

First it should be observed that despite the nickname given this verse, the word "sword" never occurs in the Qur'an—any more than "holy war" does.[4] The fact that this verse cannot be understood just on its own is clear from the reference to "forbidden months." What are they? The beginning of Surah 9 tells us. There was a sacred truce of four months whose terms were broken by "idolaters," and so Allah releases the Muslims from their commitment to the truce (9.1–2). But the idolaters who have not broken the truce are to be treated honorably:

> As for those idolaters who have honoured the treaty you [believers] made with them and who have not supported anyone against you: fulfil your agreement with them to the end of their term. God loves those who are mindful of Him. (9.4)

The context for the "sword verse" continues immediately afterward to speak of mercy toward unbelievers:

> If any one of the idolaters should seek your protection [Prophet], grant it to him so that he may hear the word of God, then take him to a place safe for him, for they are people who do not know. How could there be a treaty with God and His Messengers for idolaters?—But as for those with whom you made a treaty [*truce*] at the Sacred Mosque [*Ka'bah*], so long as they remain true to you, be true to them; God loves those who are mindful of Him. (9.6–7)

A covenantal treaty—as opposed to a simple truce—cannot be formed wherein the oath is sworn to the One God if the unbelievers do not recognize the One God. But this section says that if a treaty is turned down by idolaters who nonetheless have sought protection, they should be released to live with their own. They are the people "who do not know"—we are reminded of Jesus saying on the cross, "Father, forgive them—they clearly [*gar*] do not know what they are doing" (Lk 23.34). But specific truces can be made with the unbelievers who honor the Ka'bah for their own reasons, and those terms should be observed. Moreover, no war is justified except by a prior aggression against the warriors:

> God may still bring about affection between you and your [present enemies]—God is all powerful, God is most forgiving and merciful—and He does not forbid you to deal kindly and justly with anyone who has not fought you for your faith or driven you out of your homes. (60.7–8)[5]

So the "sword verse" used to foist on Muslims the idea of a holy war against all infidels (including Christians and Jews) proves just the opposite. It is far more forgiving and pacific than Christian heresy hunts (e.g., against Cathars) or Hebrew wars of extinction like the one against Heshbon.[6]

Coincidentally, Christians have their own often-misconstrued "sword verse," and one that actually does use the word "sword." Jesus tells his followers it is time to buy a sword (Lk 22.36). What use has Jesus for a sword when he told his followers, if they were punched on the right cheek, to offer the other cheek to be punched (Mt 5.39)? He told Pilate he would have warriors to fight for him if his reign were of this temporal order, but his reign is not of this temporal order (Jn 18.36). Jesus's real attitude to swords is expressed when Peter uses one to hack off a servant's ear. Jesus says, "Put back the sword—those taking to the sword will surely [*gar*] perish by it" (Mt 26.52). How to make sense of all these passages? Look to the entire setting of that first call for purchasing a sword (Lk 22.35–38):

He told them, "When I sent you out carrying no wallet or supply sack or shoes, did you suffer for it?" They answered, "Not at all." Then he said, "Well, now a man should carry a wallet if he has one, and a supply sack, and trade his shirt to get a sword, for the words in Scripture are coming true of me: 'He was declared an outlaw' [Is 53.12]. That prophecy, be assured [*kai gar*], is about me." And they said, "Lord, here are two swords." And he answered, "Enough of that" [*Hikanon estin*].

This passage occurs in Luke's version of the Last Supper. Jesus has just said that Satan is about to test his followers—he tells Peter he will falter, but he should recover and strengthen the others. Peter, cocky as ever, says he will never falter (Lk 22.31–34). Jesus follows these words by saying, in effect, "I am now Public Enemy Number One. I guess followers should dress like my outlaw gang, swords and all." The literal-minded disciples, as usual, don't get it. They volunteer, "Well, we have two swords," and Jesus resignedly says something like "Forget it." Luke's is not only the most humane Gospel (with the stories of the Good Samaritan, the Prodigal Son, the Good Thief, and the Believing Centurion), but the most slyly ironic.

Later Christianity, in a terrible distortion of the revealed word, used the two swords of Luke to justify papal armies, as if Jesus, not his dopier disciples, had mentioned "two swords." Some said the church had a spiritual sword (like the inner jihad Muslims talk of) and monarchs had a temporal sword to guard the church. In the twelfth century Bernard of Clairvaux wrote of Luke's swords:

Both swords belong to the church, the spiritual and the material sword—the one is to be used *for* the church, the other *by* the church. This latter sword is in the priest's hand, the former in a military hand, but only when directed by the priest who guides the emperor's hand.[7]

And in the fourteenth century a pope, Boniface VIII, said the same thing:

> One sword belongs to the church, a spiritual sword like the material one—but the latter is to be used *for* the church, while the former *by* the church—one held by the priest, the other by kings and their troops, but used only by the direction and permission of the priest.[8]

Tracing the travel out from Gospel to brute power in Christianity can help us understand a similar excursion out from the Qur'an to Islamic imperialism.

Making War Holy?

The religion of the Qur'an is a religion of peace. Can we say, therefore, that Islam is a religion of peace? That is a different matter. We can say that the religion of the New Testament is a religion of peace. But we cannot say that about Christianity, not after numberless wars of religious conquest, crusades, and inquisitions. These were not only wars against pagans and Jews and Muslims but wars against fellow Christians—Queen Mary I of England burning Protestants, Queen Elizabeth I hanging and drawing and quartering Catholics, New England Puritans hanging Quakers, Protestant crowds in the United States burning down Catholic convents. Why does religion so often veer into fanaticism? Why do the persecuted become persecutors?

Zeal is a dangerous emotion, one that often, from purest origins, runs out beyond its first object. Pair it with war—even with justified wars of self-defense—and it can become a raging flame. Clausewitz said that all war tends toward the absolute. It escalates by the "ratchetings-up" (*Wechselwirkung*) of reciprocal hostilities.[9] So the defensive war justified in the Qur'an soon became an imperial effort to impose Islam as a ruling power—this despite the warning Allah gave Muhammad on his clash with Quraysh fighters who were barring his access to the Ka'bah in 628 CE (SQ 1246–47). Some wanted the Prophet to attack Mecca, matching the disbelievers' mad fury and endangering innocent people. But Allah sent down a spirit of peace and restraint on the believers, telling them to honor the treaty with the Quraysh, even if some on the other side did not honor it (SQ 1253–55).

> In the valley of Mecca it was He who held their hands back from you and your hands back from them after He gave you the advantage over them—God sees all that you do. They were the ones who disbelieved, who barred you from the Sacred Mosque, and who prevented the offering from reaching its place of sacrifice. If there had not been among them, unknown to you, believing men and women whom you would have trampled underfoot, inadvertently incurring guilt on their account—God brings whoever He will into His mercy— if the [believers] had been clearly separated, We would have inflicted a painful punishment on the disbelievers. While the disbelievers had stirred up fury in their hearts—the fury of ignorance—God sent His tranquillity down on to His Messenger and the believers and made binding on them [their] promise to obey God, for that was more appropriate and fitting for them. God has full knowledge of all things. (48.24–26)

There were Muslims in Mecca while Muhammad's forces threatened the city. Only pagans ("idolaters") had waged war against the believers, not the Muslims in their midst. To storm the city would be to "trample underfoot" the innocent—victims of what is now called "collateral damage" or "friendly fire" or the necessities of war. The Qur'an does not bless that kind of war. Those waging it "incur guilt on their account." This was not just a directive for this one situation. Elsewhere we are given the rules of engagement—whom one can fight, and how—and they are remarkably discriminating:

> If anyone kills a believer by mistake he must free one Muslim slave and pay compensation to the victim's relatives, unless they charitably forgo it; if the victim belonged to a people at war with you but is a believer, then the compensation is only to free a believing slave; if he belonged to a people with whom you have a treaty, then compensation should be handed over to his relatives, and a believing slave set free. Anyone who lacks the means to do this must fast for two consecutive months by way of repentance to God: God is all knowing, all wise. If anyone kills a believer deliberately, the punishment for him is Hell, and there he will remain: God is angry with him, and rejects him, and has prepared a tremendous torment for him. So, you who believe, be careful when you go to fight in God's way, and do not say to someone who offers you a greeting of peace, "You are not a believer," out of a desire for the chance gains of this life—God has plenty of gains for you. You yourself were in the same position [once], but God was gracious to you, so be careful: God is fully aware of what you do. (4.92–94)

Needless to say, the tranquillity Allah sent down on the troops outside Mecca is not often maintained in the midst of hostilities.

There are many things that make religious war the most deadly kind. If our side is seen as God's cause, the other side must be anti-God, must be evil, must be Satan. It is hard to observe any truce with Satan.

So, just as the Christian empire grew by battle and slaughter, so did the Islamic empire. In either case, priests and imams found ways to twist the Gospel or the Qur'an into weird justifications for outrageous behavior. Both parties came to believe that "God wills it"—which is an egregious insult to God. The present difference between Christian and Islamic bellicosity is supposed to be that we are on two different time schedules. Christians like to think they have outgrown their medieval religious fanaticism while Islam has not. This mistakes the revanchist Muslim caliphate for the general world of Islamist believers who have repudiated it. So far from representing the majority of modern Muslims, the minority fanatics seem to be unaware of their own real traditions. To quote again Patricia Crone:

> People like Osama bin Laden and Ayman al-Zawahiri don't even seem to know their own traditions all that well. Rather, they have stripped Islam of practically everything that most Muslims consider to be their religion.[10]

Nor can we rely too readily on our own enlightened escape from medieval impulse. Professor Crone rightly suspects that there can be a secular form of jihad. She does not mention the names of Bush or Cheney, Rumsfeld or Wolfowitz, but she does not need to.

> They too tend to be eager to rescue other people by enabling them to become more like themselves: richer, freer, more democratic. What do you do when your fingers are itching to

intervene, when you have the power to do it, when you are sure you are right and you are convinced that the victims will be grateful—quite apart from the advantages that may redound to yourself from intervening?

Aren't you allowed to use force; indeed, aren't you obliged to use it? Is it right to save people against their will? Shouldn't you force them to be free? If you say yes to these questions, you are in effect a believer in jihad.[11]

No one should claim to be following the Gospel or the Qur'an when pushing forward this understanding of jihad.

NOTES

1. Muhammad Abdel Haleem, *Understanding the Qur'an: Themes and Styles* (I. B. Tauris, 2001), p. 64:

   "Holy War" does not exist as a term in Arabic, and its translation into Arabic sounds quite alien. The term which is specifically used in the Qur'an for fighting is *qital*. *Jihad* can be by argumentation (25.52), financial help or actual fighting. *Jihad* is always described in the Qur'an as *fi sabil illah* ["in the way of God"].

2. Patricia Crone, "'Jihad': Idea and History," *openDemocracy*, Apr. 30, 2007, p. 2.
3. Haleem, op. cit., p. 66.
4. Ibid., p. 68.
5. "In this context, *God does not forbid you* is understood as a positive exhortation meaning 'God wishes you to do so'" (SQ 1361).
6. Deuteronomy 2.32–34:

   Then [King] Sihon with all his people [of Heshbon] came out to meet us in battle at Jahaz, and the Lord our God delivered him into our hands; we killed him with his sons and all his people. We captured all his cities at that time and put to death everyone in the cities, men, women, and dependents; we left no survivors. (Dt 2.32–34, Num 21.35)

7. Bernard, *De Consideratione* (c 1150) 4.7.

8. Boniface VIII, *Unam Sanctam* (1301) par. 4.

9. Carl von Clausewitz, *Vom Kriege* 1.1.3.

10. Crone, op. cit., p. 7.

11. Ibid., p. 6.

CHAPTER 9

The Right Path (Shari'ah)

A tree, whose network of branches and twigs stems from the same trunk and roots; a sea, formed by the merging waters of different rivers; a variety of threads woven into a single garment; even the interlaced holes of a fishing net: these are some of the metaphors used by Muslim authors to explain the phenomenon of *ikhtilaf*, or diversity of doctrine, in Shari'a law.

—NOEL JAMES COULSON[1]

The word "shari'ah" occurs only once in the Qur'an, and there it does not mean "law." It is Allah's reassurance to Muhammad that he is traveling on the right "path" (shari'ah). There is a vast body of laws proposed or enacted under different Muslim regimes through the centuries, and they all purport to keep one on the straightest path to the supreme oasis of heaven or, more immediately, to its foretype, the well-watered Mecca. But the Qur'an does not furnish one with minute legal guidance. As Jonathan A. C. Brown writes:

The Quran is not a detailed legal manual. Only about five hundred of the book's [6,235] verses provide legal injunctions, and even on major questions such as ritual prayer, the Quran is often vague.[2]

By the time Islam acquired its earlier and later empires, the vague and sketchy elements of law in the Qur'an had been fleshed out, as it were, by *sunnah* (the Prophet's reported behavior), *ahadith* (the Prophet's reported sayings), *qiyas* (analogical extensions), *ijma* (scholars' consensus), and the demands of rule under the various regimes—which was like the growth of canon law under the various empires of the Catholic church. So when state legislatures in the United States ban Shari'ah law, what are they banning, specifically? If a foreign country were to ban Christian law, what law would they mean? There are many bodies of Christian laws, accumulated over a long and contentious history. Would it be canon law? If so, which body of law from which era would they be singling out? Or the Westminster Confession? The Thirty-Nine Articles? The Canons of Dordt? The Ecclesiastical Ordinances?

Or how would one ban Jewish law? What would be outlawed? Deuteronomy? Halakha? Israeli government law? Even the latter, as still contemporary and enforced, is not a simple or single matter. According to an extensive and nuanced 2016 survey by the Pew Research Center, Israel's Jewish population is divided into four groups, with widely varying attitudes on the relation of civil law to Jewish law.[3] The groups are Haredi (ultra-Orthodox, 8 percent of the population), Dati (religious, 10 percent), Masorti (traditional, 23 percent), and Hiloni (secular, 40 percent). The first two rarely socialize or intermarry with the last two. The first two oppose the operation of public transport on the Sabbath and the military conscription of their fellow believers, and think Halakha should prevail over the civil law. The last two groups oppose these policies. Judging Shari'ah from the point of view of ISIS would be like judging Halakha in terms of the minority Haredi or Dati Jews. There are traditional and secular Muslims, with their own attitudes toward Shari'ah, just as there are Masorti and Hiloni among Jews. In fact, something like the Pew poll taxonomy of different attitudes toward Jewish law can be laid out for Muslim attitudes. Jonathan A. C. Brown finds four main divisions in Islamic observance— Islamic Modernism, Modernist Salafism, Traditionalist Salafism, and Late Sunni Traditionalism.[4] Just as with the Jewish schools of thought, there are some overlaps of the different divisions, and further subdivisions in any one of them.

And behind those differing approaches in our time there are long scholarly traditions of Islamic law. The majority Sunni Muslims have four main schools of Shari'ah law, and the minority Shia have three schools.[5] One cannot generalize even within these two branches, much less in the two of them combined. As Noel Coulson says of the minority branch, with its three schools:

> Since these three groups all possess their own distinct legal systems, the term "Shi'ite law" can only be used by way of the broadest generalisation and is often, without further qualification, as meaningless as the term "Sunnite law."[6]

One or another of these schools of interpretation is preferred according to where one lives. The four Sunni schools predominate in these areas:

Hanafi: Arab world and South Asia

Hanbali: Saudi Arabia

Maliki: North, Central, and West Africa

Shaf'i: East Africa and Southeast Asia[7]

How, in this situation, can so many legislatures in the United States outlaw Shari'ah law? What forms, examples, or excerpts of laws, from which period or locale, are they identifying, in order to ban them? Some seem to think the fanatical punishments dealt out by the self-proclaimed Islamic State—beheadings, maimings, shamings, degradation, the killing of civilians—are the essence of Shari'ah law, though the vast majority of Muslims, and their most learned teachers, do not recognize these as bearing any relation to the Qur'an. It is true that the Qur'an has elements of the lex talionis ("law of redress," or retaliation):

> Cut off the hands of thieves, whether they are man or woman, as punishment for what they have done—a deterrent from God: God is almighty and wise. But if anyone repents after his wrongdoing and makes amends, God will accept his repentance: God is most forgiving, most merciful. (5.38–39)

The possibility of "making amends" seems to indicate that restoration of the stolen goods, perhaps with an added penalty, can occur before legal conviction of the criminal act and legal execution. The last forum here, as always, is that of God's mercy.

We should remember that many ancient codes are often based on the lex talionis principle, the one proclaimed by W. S. Gilbert's Mikado:

> *My object all sublime*
> *I shall achieve in time,*
> *To make the punishment fit the crime.*

This is called the "eye-for-an-eye" principle, from the Jewish scripture:

> Whenever hurt is done, you shall give life for life, eye for eye, tooth for tooth, hand for hand, foot for foot, burn for burn, bruise for bruise, wound for wound. (Ex 21.23–25)

The Qur'an has a similar punishment ("life for life") for murder (2.178). It is shockingly physical in its punishment of those who persecute Muslims or "spread corruption in the land" (presumably undermining belief in the One God, a sin only pagans can commit, not Jews or Christians).

> Those who wage war against God and His Messenger and strive to spread corruption in the land should be punished by death, crucifixion, the amputation of an alternate hand and foot, or banishment from the land: a disgrace for them in this world, and then a terrible punishment in the Hereafter, unless they repent before you overpower them—in that case bear in mind that God is forgiving and merciful. (5.33–34)

There would be much debate down through the years about what would constitute "corruption in the land." But even here there is room for forgiveness before "you overpower them"—that is, convict them of the crime. We saw in chapter 7 that the Muslim punishment for adultery (flogging) was less severe than the Jewish one (stoning)—and neither is honored by the main body of Jews or Muslims today.

We should remember that the harsh physical punishments proclaimed in the seventh-century Qur'an are not more gory than those imposed in sixteenth-century England, where ear cropping and other appropriate amputations were common. When John Stubbs wrote a pamphlet criticizing Queen Elizabeth for entertaining the prospect of marrying a Catholic prince, he and his publisher were sentenced to have their right hands cut off.[8] This was a common enough penalty that the proper mode of execution was established— a great cleaver was placed on the wrist, then a giant mallet pounded it through the bones and nerves. This, it will be seen, was a kind of miniature guillotine *avant la lettre.*

But actual beheading in Elizabeth's time could be far more cruel. It took a kind of evil genius to invent a death by hanging, drawing, and quartering—the penalty prescribed for traitors, and especially for Jesuits and other priests who were deemed to be honoring Pope Pius V's excommunication of the queen. The condemned was hanged, then cut down before he died so he could see the "drawing" out of his bowels, after which his arms, legs, and head were lopped off. This was conceived as a didactic talio, directed at the head and heart that devised the treason and then the limbs that tried to carry it out.

Lest we think that Elizabethan times are too removed from us to count as a civilized period, we should remember that an American body, in the period of our Revolution, proposed some lex talionis elements in the adjustments we first made to British law. Thomas Jefferson, the chairman of a committee charged with revising the laws for Virginia's use, submitted this proposal:

> Whosoever shall be guilty of Rape, Polygamy, or Sodomy with man or woman shall be punished, if a man, by castration, if a woman, by cutting through the cartilage of her nose a hole of one half diameter at the least.[9]

The talio principle is observed when adultery is punished by removal of the male penis as the instrument by which the act was performed

152 WHAT THE QUR'AN MEANT

and removal of the female beauty that provided temptation to that organ.

It is true that English and American laws have outgrown the attitudes that called for such literal justice, while the Islamic State wants to revert to its medieval conditions. But that is a minority effort among Muslims. It would have a certain American parallel, even today, if fundamentalists like the Christian Reconstructionists, inspired by Rousas John Rushdoony, got their way. They want to revive laws from Deuteronomy and Leviticus, including the death penalty for adulterers, fornicators, homosexuals, idolaters, apostates, and blasphemers. Even the state of Israel does not observe Deuteronomy or Leviticus this way.

Though there is always danger that religious documents can be read literally in totally different social contexts, all but a few Mormons have given up the multiple wives of their founders—as Jews have given up on the multiple wives of Abraham, David, and Solomon. Jefferson himself soon gave up on castration as a legal penalty. It would be as obtuse to blame today's Jews for genocide at Deuteronomy 20.16–18, or today's Mormons for polygamy, or today's Christians for slaughtering Cathari, as to blame today's Muslims for the lex talionis actions of the so-called Islamic State—even though there are some revanchist Mormons who still marry multiple wives, some Christians who call for stoning adulterers, and some Muslims who are trying to restore a caliphate that mutilated for punishment. As noted, the terrorists in modern Islam are not knowledgeable of their own religion in either profession or practice, and most scholars and leaders of Islam denounce them authoritatively.

The Westerners who describe Islam as cruel and violent are partnering with the distorters of the religion. Both the Muslim terrorists and some Western foes think of Shari'ah law mainly in terms of the penal code, even though that is a very minor aspect of the Qur'an. The few verses devoted to severe punishment are applicable only in legitimate governments ruled by Muslims—of which there are none today. ISIS (or ISIL) has no claim to legitimacy either as a religion or as a state. Its adherents are the equivalent of Christian Reconstructionists. Olivier Roy points out the folly of taking fundamentalists as the spokespersons for a whole religion:

> Although the current strategic context may lead young men to choose to identify themselves with an imaginary community and join the jihad, it is having the deeper and more long-range result of leading Muslims, moderates and neofundamentalists alike, to rethink the way in which they are integrated into Western societies, by recognizing that the radicals have distorted the political imaginative structures they hold in common.[10]

Some American legislators seem to think Shari'ah is nothing but a penal code whereas there is little mention of that in the Qur'an. Most of the book dwells on religious duty and moral conduct. And most of the rules of conduct have to do with matters like commerce and marriage, which I will discuss in the next two chapters. But the basic moral duties of observant Muslims have to do with religion, and these duties are the basic ones of all monotheistic faiths. Edward Gibbon, who was brilliant at discerning the core message of religions, before the multiple distortions and abuses that all religions suffer from, put the heart of the matter incisively. He was not a friend of religion, but he was fair in stating a religion's claims.

> The precepts of Mahomet himself inculcate a more simple and rational piety [than the pagan one]: prayer, fasting, and

alms are the religious duties of a Musulman; and he is encouraged to hope that prayer will carry him half way to God, fasting will bring him to the door of his palace, and alms will gain him admittance.[11]

A contemporary Muslim scholar could not put the point more succinctly—that the "acts of worship [are] such as prayer, fasting, almsgiving."[12] The three great duties—prayer, fasting, alms—are in a climactic order of importance. Charity to the poor, zakat, is the loftiest duty, the one with most merit. In Gibbon's words:

> The Koran repeatedly inculcates, not as a merit, but as a strict and indispensable duty, the relief of the indigent and unfortunate. Mahomet, perhaps, is the only lawgiver who has defined the precise measure of charity: the standard may vary with the degree and nature of property, as it consists either in money, in corn or cattle, in fruits or merchandise; but the Musulman does not accomplish the law, unless he bestows a *tenth* of his revenue; and if his conscience accuses him of fraud or extortion, the tenth, under the idea of restitution, is enlarged to a *fifth*. Benevolence is the foundation of justice, since we are forbid to injure those whom we are bound to assist. A prophet may reveal the secrets of heaven and of futurity; but in his moral precepts he can only repeat the lessons of our own hearts.[13]

Needless to say, these basic duties are not forbidden by the governments of Western democracies. Then what are the state legislatures in America so afraid of that they are banning Shari'ah law (what little they know of it)? And for what practices of Shari'ah are Muslims asking permission? Actually, what is desired is not so much permission as noninterference. They want for instance to conduct their own marriages, divorces, and interments. Catholics and Jews in America regulate their own practices of this sort without any conflict with the law.

Aside from polygamy, which both have given up, Muslims are as free to regulate their religious practices as the Mormons are. Muslim laws against incest are stricter than the state's, so they can be followed without ever getting near the boundaries drawn by government. The commerce rules of Islam are stricter than those of the state. Private contracts, rules of usury, can be conducted within the looser guidelines of the political society Muslims live in. This is what is happening around the world with the peaceful communities of Muslims.

As Olivier Roy points out, the modern secular state does not forbid religious practice. It allows it, and feels authorized only to keep the peace within and between denominations. In America, that means protecting mosques, allowing hijabs, helping communities deal with their own extremists. The cure for reversion to violent ways by a minority is encouragement of good relations with the majority. The obstacle to such cooperation comes from the odd union of fundamentalist Muslims and critics of Islam who think only its harshest unchanging version is authentic, even though the best Muslim scholars, like the best Jewish and Christian scholars, see development of doctrine as the true spirit of Moses or Jesus or Muhammad. As Roy writes:

In both cases [of extremism] we are dealing with what I would call the essentialist position, consisting of seeing in Islam a fixed and timeless system of thought. Critics of Islam and Muslim fundamentalists are mirrors of each other, and each corroborates the other in the view of Islam that they share, merely with the signs [positive or negative] reversed.[14]

Critics, that is, see as negative what literalists see as positive. In the same way, enemies of Christianity see as its faults what its fundamentalists promote as its virtues—e.g., hell for people who practice contraception, abortion, religious pluralism, and other things forbidden in "tradition" but not in the Gospel. Quoting Roy again:

> Countering this [violent] approach are reformist, liberal, or simply moderate Muslim thinkers and theologians, who rely on the abundant theological and philosophical debates in Islam at the time of the Umayyad (661–750) and Abbasid (750–1258) dynasties—for example, the rationalist Mutazilite school (whereas, by definition, fundamentalists think of this period as the one when Islam was corrupted by Greek philosophy). These thinkers are, of course, spread over a wide range of opinions, ranging from conservative moderates, theologically very orthodox but very flexible with regard to the possible consequences of dogma in political, social, and cultural fields, to real reformers, who think that the theological question must be reexamined.[15]

This neglected side of the Muslims' own tradition was referred to by the Islamic scholar Patricia Crone in 2007:

> The Muslim record of tolerance is generally good. (Obviously there are plenty of examples of persecution of one kind or another; [but] that religious minorities generally speaking did better under Muslim than under Christian rule under premodern conditions nonetheless remains true, however hackneyed the claim has become.)[16]

There is little of what was later called Shari'ah law in the Qur'an, and practically nothing of constitutional theory, since Muhammad was not commissioned by Allah as a ruler. He is told repeatedly that he is not a "guardian" or "watcher" or "keeper" of his people, but solely a messenger.[17] It is his duty to convey the proclamation exactly as it was dictated to him. It is true that a labyrinthine growth of ever-more-minute rules would grow up. Precisely because the Qur'an is so little prone to such rule making, it was supplemented by qiyas, sunnah, ahadith, and ijma. These could be endlessly juggled or pitted against each other. A hadith (saying) of weak authority could be propped up by an ijma (consensus).[18] It became a point of pride with some teachers to add vast amounts of learned lumber to this accumulation. Ahmad ibn-Hanbal is said to have collected eighty thousand ahadith.[19] This dense overgrowth of legalisms might be compared to the ramifying of technicalities and legalistic subdistinctions in late medieval Christian Scholasticism. Neither of these vast structures is reflected in the Gospel or the Qur'an.

Nonetheless, we can see how some minimal amplification of the Qur'an was necessary from the outset. Take the example of cutting off the hand of a thief. Would that apply to someone who took a few dates? If not, what amount constitutes "theft" in the Qur'anic sense? And should analogy apply the principle of talio to other cases not mentioned in the Qur'an? And does the wholesale desertion of even the hand amputation by modern Muslims amount to a kind of naskh? There is ample room for debate in conscientious observance of the Qur'an. But we should remember that the text of the Qur'an allows for repentance and forgiveness in the case of theft—in fact, with all sins. This is the greatest point of contrast with some modern invocations of Shari'ah by foe or friend, presenting the spirit of Islamic law as fierce and vengeful. Nothing could be falser.

It is a text of constant mercy and forgiving:

Say, "[God says], My servants who have harmed yourselves by your own excess, do not despair of God's mercy. God forgives all sins. He is truly the Most Forgiving, the Most Merciful. (39.53)

Anyone who does evil or wrongs his own soul and then asks God for forgiveness will find Him most forgiving and merciful. (4.110)

Since Allah is forgiving, his followers should be so, too, giving alms even to sinners:

Those who have been graced with bounty and plenty should not swear that they will [no longer] give to kinsmen, the poor, those who emigrated in God's way: let them pardon and forgive. Do you not wish that God should forgive you? God is most forgiving and merciful. (24.22)

This spirit of forgiveness is like that of the prophet Jesus:

I tell you, love your foes and pray for your oppressors, that you may be children to your Father of the Heavens, who lifts the sun up over bad people and good, and rains upon the just and the unjust. (Mt 5.44–45)

It is not accidental that all the surahs but one begin with the Basmalah:

In the Name of God, the Lord of Mercy, the Giver of Mercy

God is merciful not only to sinners who repent, but to his followers
who find their duties hard to carry out, or who err accidentally:

> He will not call you to account for oaths you have uttered
> unintentionally, but He will call you to account for what you
> mean in your hearts. God is most forgiving and forbearing.
> (2.225)

> No one should be burdened with more than they can bear.
> (2.233)

The duties are fungible. For one who cannot make the Hijra pilgrimage or shave his head to celebrate that, God says to substitute
more prayer or alms.

> Complete the pilgrimages, major and minor, for the sake of
> God. If you are prevented [from doing so], then [send] what-
> ever offering for sacrifice you can afford, and do not shave
> your heads until the offering has reached the place of sacri-
> fice. If any of you is ill, or has an ailment of the scalp, he
> should compensate by fasting or feeding the poor, or offering
> sacrifice. (2.196)

The fungibility of duties can apply to penances done for offenses:

> God does not take you [to task] for what is thoughtless in
> your oaths, only for your binding oaths: the atonement for
> breaking an oath is to feed ten poor people with food equiv-
> alent to what you would normally give your own families, or
> to clothe them, or to set free a slave—if a person cannot find
> the means, he should fast for three days. (5.89)[20]

One of the offenses men can commit is *zihar*, "shunning," rejecting a wife without divorcing her, which leaves her without knowledge of her status.[21] A man who does that and then tries to resume the marriage is wronging his wife, an offense for which there are fungible punishments:

> Those of you who say such a thing to their wives, then go back on what they have said, must free a slave before the couple may touch one another again—this is what you are commanded to do, and God is fully aware of what you do— but anyone who does not have the means should fast continuously for two months before they touch each other, and anyone unable to do this should feed sixty needy people. (58.3–4)

Even penitence takes the form of alternative charities, all calibrated to a person's capacities.

> For those who can fast only with extreme difficulty, there is a way to compensate—feed a needy person. . . . God wants ease for you, not hardship. . . . If My servants ask you about Me, I am near. I respond to those who call Me. (2.184–86)

This, too, sounds like some words of the prophet Jesus:

> Approach me, you who are weary and weighed down, and I will respite you. Take on yourselves my yoke and become my disciples [*mathetai*], since I am gentle and yielding at heart and you will find respite for your spirit, since my yoke is rewarding [*chrestos*] and its weight is light. (Mt 11.28–30)

Some Muslims' piling on of harsh demands and punishments that are not in the Qur'an resembles the rebuke of Jesus to the Pharisees of his time:

> They lash together heavy burdens for men's backs, while lifting not a single finger to lift them. (Mt 23.4)

This is a recurrent theme of the Qur'an:

> God does not wish to place any burden on you. (5.6)

> God wishes to lighten your burden; man was created weak. (4.28)

> We do not burden any soul with more than it can bear. (6.152)

> God does not burden any soul with more than it can bear. (2.286)

> We do not burden any soul with more than it can bear. (7.42)

> We do not burden any soul with more than it can bear. (23.62)

NOTES

1. N. J. Coulson, *A History of Islamic Law* (Edinburgh University Press, 1964), p. 86.
2. Jonathan A. C. Brown, *Hadith: Muhammad's Legacy in the Medieval and Modern World* (Oneworld, 2009), p. 150.
3. "Israel's Religiously Divided Society," Pew Research Center, Mar. 8, 2016, pp. 1–21.
4. Brown, op. cit., pp. 243–63.

5. Coulson, op. cit. The Sunni schools are:

Hanafi
Maliki
Shaf'i
Hanbali

The Shia schools are:

Ithna-'ashari ("Twelvers")
Isma'ili
Zaydi

The Twelvers can be further divided into:

Ja'fari
Akhbari

6. Ibid., p. 106.

7. John L. Esposito, *What Everyone Needs to Know About Islam*, 2nd ed. (Oxford University Press, 2011), p. 47.

8. Lloyd E. Berry, ed., *John Stubbs's "Gaping Gulf," with Letters and Other Relevant Documents* (University Press of Virginia, 1968).

9. *Papers of Thomas Jefferson*, vol. 2, ed. Julian P. Boyd (Princeton University Press, 1950), p. 498.

10. Olivier Roy, *Secularism Confronts Islam*, trans. George Holoch (Columbia University Press, 2007), p. 94.

11. Edward Gibbon, *The History of the Decline and Fall of the Roman Empire*, ed. David Womersley (Penguin, 1994), vol. 3, p. 184.

12. Ahmad Muhammad al-Tayyib, "The Quran as Source of Islamic Law," SQ 1701.

13. Gibbon, op. cit., p. 187.

14. Roy, op. cit., p. 43.

15. Ibid.

16. Patricia Crone, "'Jihad': Idea and History," *openDemocracy*, Apr. 30, 2007.

17. See 3.20, 4.80, 6.66, 6.104, 6.107, 13.40, 17.54, 25.43, 29.18, 39.41, 42.48.

18. Brown, op. cit., p. 258. This reminds me of a New Testament scholar who compared the three Synoptic Gospels to three drunks going home arm in arm—when one is toppling, the others prop him up.

19. Coulson, op. cit., p. 71.

20. Freeing a slave is atonement as well for different kinds of manslaughter:

If anyone kills a believer by mistake he must free one Muslim slave and pay compensation to the victim's relatives, unless they charitably forgo it; if the victim belonged to a people at war with you but is a believer, then the compensation is only to free a believing slave; if he belonged to a people with whom you have a treaty, then compensation should be handed over to his relatives, and a believing slave set free. (4.92)

21. The offensive form of shunning uses the words "treat her as if she were his mother's back," to which Muhammad bitingly says:

Their only mothers are those who gave birth to them. (58.2)

CHAPTER 10

Commerce

The economic world reflected in the Qur'an is not agrarian or industrial but commercial. Mecca was an inland entrepôt. It dealt with merchant caravans coming and going, which involved the promises of payment for incoming goods and investment to ensure that outgoing caravans would have the means of reaching their goal. It is an inland version of the seaside mart depicted in *The Merchant of Venice*, where the comings and goings of merchant vessels resemble the caravan traffic of Mecca. Both worlds depend on the exchange of goods, with different currencies of exchange. These are centers of financial risk (Arabic *gharar*), and they are both concerned with the subject of usury, of people making money from the vulnerability of certain risks.

Mecca when Muhammad's revelations began was not a municipality where all tribes could rely on the arbitrations of a neutral and stable state, so guarantees had to be constructed for each transaction. Muhammad had been the manager of his first wife's commercial interests, and the instructions on Muslim business dealings show a hands-on expertise. The deal should be written down and witnessed by multiple persons whom the agents know and trust. These ad hoc social forms are honor-bound to be self-policing.

You who believe, when you contract a debt for a stated term, put it down in writing: have a scribe write it down justly between you. No scribe should refuse to write: let him write as God has taught him, let the debtor dictate, and let him fear God, his Lord, and not diminish [the debt] at all. If the debtor is feeble-minded, weak, or unable to dictate, then let his guardian dictate justly. Call in two men as witnesses. If two men are not there, then call one man and two women out of those you approve as witnesses, so that if one of the two women should forget the other can remind her. Let the witnesses not refuse when they are summoned. Do not disdain to write the debt down, be it small or large, along with the time it falls due: this way is more equitable in God's eyes, more reliable as testimony, and more likely to prevent doubts arising between you. But if the merchandise is there and you hand it over, there is no blame on you if you do not write it down. Have witnesses present whenever you trade with one another, and let no harm be done to either scribe or witness, for if you did cause them harm, it would be a crime on your part. Be mindful of God, and He will teach you: He has full knowledge of everything. (2.282)

If the trading takes place outside of Mecca—if, for instance, a party is traveling with one of the caravans or going on pilgrimage— he must form a structure adapted to the circumstances.

If you are on a journey, and cannot find a scribe, something should be handed over as security, but if you decide to trust one another, then let the one who is trusted fulfil his trust; let him be mindful of God, his Lord. Do not conceal evidence: anyone who does so has a sinful heart, and God is fully aware of everything you do. (2.283)

Anyone cheating another person is in effect stealing from God, since all things he made are his property:

> Whatever is in the heavens and in the earth belongs to God and, whether you reveal or conceal your thoughts, God will call you to account for them. (2.284)

God is a great accountant. Those who are weighing out what is due should reflect how God, in ordering the universe, weighs and balances all things. Human beings, by keeping tidy accounts, become imitators of God.

> The sun and the moon follow their calculated courses; the plants and the trees submit to His designs; He has raised up the sky. He has set the balance, so that you may not exceed in the balance: weigh with justice and do not fall short in the balance. (55.5–9)

This picture of God's precise balancing of everything in the universe is like the passage in the apocryphal Book of Wisdom:

> You have ordered all things by measure, number, and weight. (Ws 11.20)

This was a favorite verse of Augustine, who found Trinitarian meanings in it.[1]

Muhammad cannot insist enough on accuracy of measurement. It is the test of individual integrity and the bond of honest community.

> Give full measure when you measure, and weigh with accurate scales. (17.35)

Give full measure: do not sell others short. Weigh with correct scales: do not deprive people of what is theirs. (26.181–83)

Give full measure and weight and do not undervalue people's goods. (7.85)

Woe to those who give short measure, who demand of other people full measure for themselves, but when it is they who weigh or measure for others give less than they should. (83.1–3)

Do not give short measure nor short weight. I see you are prospering, but I fear you will have torment on an overwhelming Day. My people, in fairness, give full measure and weight. Do not withhold from people things that are rightly theirs. (11.84–85)

The model for true believers in Allah is the honest merchant. The rule of all morality is "measure for measure," as in the Gospel of Matthew:

The decision you render about others will be rendered in return about you, and the way you measure out treatment of others will measure how you are treated. (Mt 7.2)

Control of your monetary dealings is an indication of self-control in general, and it gives the ground for other just acts.

Do not eat up your property wrongfully, nor use it to bribe judges, intending sinfully and knowingly to eat up parts of other people's property. (2.188)

Muslims' whole economic system depends on integrity. The great enemy of that would be the mutual deception involved in taking unearned gains from the system. That basic breaking of the financial social contract goes by the name *riba* in the Qur'an, usually translated as "usury." But if usury just means taking interest on loans, the translation is inadequate. Caner Dagli points out that *riba* means one of two things in the Qur'an—punishing late payments cruelly, or misleading others in the statement of values. The harsh penalty for late payments is condemned in this verse:

> You who believe, do not consume usurious interest, doubled and redoubled. (3.130)

Dagli writes of this verse:

> A deferment on already existing loans . . . often led to doubling of the principal in a year and then redoubling when the deferment period expired and another deferment became necessary. . . . A debtor could eventually lose all his possessions to the creditor through the doubling and redoubling mentioned in the Qur'an. (SQ 120)

Misleading people about values occurs when one counts as less or more what is being traded. If the same amount of shoddy goods is equated with that amount of pristine goods, one is stealing the difference in the two values. If one is trading one-on-one and face-to-face, the values of the traded objects should be equal. But things get more complicated when trade is across time or space. The shipping costs of goods must be taken into account, and the loss of the use of the thing until payment comes due. Dagli explains the Qur'an rule:

In such a transaction the time factor creates an inequality; an ounce of gold is worth more now than in the future because one loses the ability to use it in the meantime, and this disparity is a "surplus" (which applies in matters of trade, not charitable loans). (SQ 120)

To ignore the time or space effects would itself create an inequality in the trade, so that cannot be the forbidden *riba*. The rule is fairness at both ends of the exchange, as calculated with best knowledge and goodwill. Risk must be factored in.

Since risk is always present in some form in all honest business transactions, [Muslim] jurists allowed certain kinds of transaction, such as forward sales on agricultural products, which, though they amount to sales in the future of nonexistent items and involve risk, were allowed because of their social and economic benefits and also in many cases necessity. Forward sales of crops were practiced in Madinah (see v. 282), though the Prophet set strict conditions on them, as did later jurists following his example, so that they would not be made to bear excessive risk or become a cover for the forbidden *riba*. (SQ 121)

As always, the integrity of the merchant should be manifest in the use of honest witnesses and written guarantees. The disparities should be proved not to be excessive. One of the great purposes of trade is to equip a believer for one of his three principal tasks—the giving of alms. How can one be virtuous in gifts of money he has won by vicious practices?

Those who give, out of their own possessions, by night and by day, in private and in public, will have their reward with their

Lord: no fear for them, nor will they grieve. But those who take usury will rise up on the Day of Resurrection like someone tormented by Satan's touch. That is because they say, "Trade and usury [*riba*] are the same," but God has allowed trade and forbidden usury. (2.274–76)

Since returning usurious gains would involve tracing old deals with dispersed people and goods, there should be an amnesty over past transactions, so long as there is no relapse.

Whoever, on receiving God's warning, stops taking usury may keep his past gains—God will be his judge—but whoever goes back to usury will be an inhabitant of the Fire, there to remain. God blights usury, but blesses charitable deeds with multiple increase. (2.276)

Those able to earn riches by money should share their wealth with those unable to trade (or to go on pilgrimage) though they observe the other principal duty (to pray):

[Give] to those needy who are wholly occupied in God's way and cannot travel in the land [for trade]. The unknowing might think them rich because of their self-restraint, but you will recognize them by their characteristic of not begging persistently. God is well aware of any good you give. (2.273)

As one may not trade inferior goods for superior ones in commerce, one cannot give less than good things in charity, fearing that you will become poor by giving your own goods:

You who believe, give charitably from the good things you have acquired and that We have produced for you from the earth. Do not seek to give the bad things that you yourself would only accept with your eyes closed: remember that God is self-sufficient, worthy of all praise. Satan threatens you with the prospect of poverty and commands you to do foul deeds; God promises you His forgiveness and His abundance: God is limitless and all knowing, and He gives wisdom to whoever He will. Whoever is given wisdom has truly been given much good, but only those with insight bear this in mind. Whatever you may give, or vow to give, God knows it well, and those who do wrong will have no one to help them. (2.267–70)

The virtuous person uses his well-gotten gains to do good works. The highest of these are feeding the poor and freeing slaves. This is the best kind of zeal (jihad) in trying times:

What will explain to you what the steep path is? It is to free a slave, to feed at a time of hunger an orphaned relative or a poor person in distress, and to be one of those who believe and urge one another to steadfastness and compassion. Those who do this will be on the right-hand side, but those who disbelieve in Our revelations will be on the left-hand side, and the Fire will close in on them. (90.12–20)

Doing these good works can free one from the consequences of unintended wrongs. I quote again a passage on the rules of war, now to connect it with doing good works like freeing slaves:

If anyone kills a believer by mistake he must free one Muslim slave and pay compensation to the victim's relatives, unless they charitably forgo it; if the victim belonged to a people at war with you but is a believer, then the compensation is only to free a believing slave; if he belonged to a people with whom you have a treaty, then compensation should be handed over to his relatives, and a believing slave set free. Anyone who lacks the means to do this must fast for two consecutive months by way of repentance to God: God is all knowing, all wise. If anyone kills a believer deliberately, the punishment for him is Hell, and there he will remain: God is angry with him, and rejects him, and has prepared a tremendous torment for him. So, you who believe, be careful when you go to fight in God's way, and do not say to someone who offers you a greeting of peace, "You are not a believer," out of a desire for the chance gains of this life—God has plenty of gains for you. You yourself were in the same position [once], but God was gracious to you, so be careful: God is fully aware of what you do. (4.92–94)

The ultimate insurance against *riba* is the intent of any real believer to use his material gains for spiritual striving, the ultimate jihad.

NOTES

1. Augustine plumbed this verse for deeper meanings throughout his entire writing career. See James J. O'Donnell, Augustine, *Confessions* (Oxford University Press, 1992), vol. 2, pp. 293–95.

CHAPTER 11

Women: Plural Marriage

Discussion of women in the Qur'an often treats tardily or peripherally what is mostly called polygamy. But the real subject is not polygamy (multiple marriages) but polygyny (multiple wives) as opposed to polyandry (multiple husbands). I can see why modern Muslims downplay the importance of multiple wives in the Qur'an. Like Mormons, the progressives among them consider polygyny a dead letter, a remnant of the past not quite forgotten but healthily forgettable. But polygyny radiates an influence through all the treatments of women in the Qur'an, even parts that have no obvious connection with it. It helps explain the most controversial verse about women, the one that instructs a husband (under certain conditions) to hit his wife:

> If you fear high-handedness from your wives, remind them [of the teachings of God], then ignore them in bed, then hit them. If they obey you, you have no right to act against them: God is most high and great. (4.34)

This gives an escalating sequence of directives. There are three stages: First, teach the woman what God demands of her. If that does not work, then boycott her bed. If that, too, is ineffectual—if she continues in her disobedience—then hit her. It is this third stage that is most discomfiting. Naturally, it gets the most extensive commentary (most of it extenuating). That does deserve full investigation, and I will take it up in my next chapter. But people say little about the second directive, to go on a one-man sex strike to bring her around.

We are familiar with a woman's ability to get "a headache" when she does not want sex. We even know about Lysistrata's organization of a citywide withdrawal by women from sex in the comedy by Aristophanes. But what leverage is given a man if he withdraws from sexual engagement? Is his wife supposed to be so hungry for sex that she will do anything to get it? This seems more like a male fantasy than a shrewd instruction maneuver from Allah. I believe that the force of this directive becomes clear only in a context of polygyny.

Withdrawing from one's wife in a bevy of co-wives would be a noticeable sign of disapproval, especially in Muhammad's maximum total of thirteen wives or concubines. A wife neglected may lose any extra advantages that come from having, actually or potentially, the husband's heir. Co-wives may scheme to reduce the influence of the neglected one, or of her offspring (if any, even potentially). We will learn that such scheming took place in Muhammad's household, and Allah's instructions on sex are often issued in this context.

What one might call the politics of the harem is an important part of all polygynous societies, including those of the Old Testament. "Harem" has become a word now discouraged because of "Orientalist" romanticizing or demonizing of seraglios—the picture of a great sultan or pasha with an extensive horde of sex slaves. But it is hard to find another word for any group of wives kept by one husband in a controlled environment, so for quickest reference I'll sometimes use the word "harem," while insistently renouncing all its *Arabian Nights* suggestions. Allah orders Muhammad's followers to keep their wives to a modest number (generally, under four), though the Prophet is allowed more, for his special circumstances. Not only do more wives demand greater riches to support them (against Muhammad's ideal of modest possessions), but they require greater efforts to treat them equitably (which Allah also commands). Even two wives can be contenders against each other, as we learn from Jewish polygyny:

> When a man has two wives, one loved and the other unloved, if they both bear him sons, and the son of the unloved wife is the elder, then, when the day comes for him to divide his property among his sons, he shall not treat the son of the loved wife as his first-born, in contempt of his true first-born, the son of the unloved wife. He shall recognize the rights of his first-born, the son of the unloved wife, and give him a double share of all that he possesses; for he was the first-fruits of his manhood, and the right of the first-born is his. (Dt 21.15–17)

Admittedly, the Jewish example draws on a general teaching that the firstfruits of anything belong to the Lord. But we can assume that polygyny would pit the interests of wives and offspring against each other in Muslim harems. For instance, when urging good Muslims to care for orphans (Muhammad had been a young orphan), the Prophet says one might have to add wives—or slaves, or both—to help with the orphans' care. The text only hints at the competitive pressures this might entail:

> If you fear that you will not deal fairly with orphan girls, you may marry whichever [other] women seem good to you, two, three, or four. If you fear you cannot be equitable [to them],

then marry only one [*more*], or your slaves(s): that is more
likely to make you avoid bias. (4.3)

Polygyny poses for the husband tasks diplomatic, political, and
economic. One must try to be a benevolent ruler, in terms of affec-
tion, justice, and finances.

Husbands should take good care of their wives. (4.34)

The Qur'an admits, later in the same chapter, that perfect impar-
tiality is impossible:

You will never be able to treat your wives with equal fairness, however much you desire to do so, but do not ignore one
wife altogether, leaving her suspended [between marriage
and divorce]. If you make amends and remain conscious of
God, He is most forgiving and merciful. (4.129)

To manage a marriage wisely took careful use of resources,
emotional and physical and, in the broad sense, social—in accord
with one's duties and standing in society. As Maria Massi Dakake
says: "The just treatment of both orphans and wives is more likely
when a man is not overburdened with dependents" (SQ 190). The
Old Testament also warns against taking more wives than one can
support. A ruler in Israel who took more wives than he could support might wish to go back for more of the Pharaoh's riches in
Egypt:

He shall not acquire many horses, nor, to add to his horses,
shall he cause the people to go back to Egypt, for this is what
the Lord said to you, "You shall never go back that way." He
shall not acquire many wives and so be led astray; nor shall he

acquire great quantities of silver and gold for himself. (Dt 17.16–17)

Of course, Solomon was rich enough to have as many horses (for his fabled stables) and wives as he wanted. He is condemned not for the number of his wives but for entertaining their foreign beliefs:

He had seven hundred wives, who were princesses, and three hundred concubines, and they turned his heart from the truth. (1 Kgs 11.3)

Muhammad was no Solomon, though he did have thirteen wives (two marriages were unconsummated) and two concubines, and various women slaves.[1] And, like Solomon, he contracted marriages for diplomatic purposes. Like some Western monarchs, he had no male heirs (his two sons died as infants) and he had to rely on his own marriages and those of his four daughters to secure a legacy—and even then, division over the succession led to the lasting split between Sunni and Shia believers. Jonathan A. C. Brown sees the logic in certain of these marriages:

Muhammad married the daughters of Abu Bakr and Umar and married his own daughters to Uthman and Ali. These four men were the first four rulers of the Muslim state after the Prophet's death. Muhammad also married the daughter of Abu Sufyan as well as the sister of Abbas' wife, Maymuna (who was also the aunt of Khalid bin al-Walid). Abu Sufyan's son Mu'awiya founded the Umayyad caliphate after Ali's death in 660 CE, and Khalid was a leading general of the Muslim armies. The Prophet's marriages and those of his family thus helped create the network that provided the leadership of the Muslim community in the century after Muhammad's death.[2]

He also married the widows of his companions who had fallen in battle, to give them honored status.

Muhammad's marriages were not trouble-free. In fact, much of the Qur'an's view of women is revealed by what Allah tells Muhammad to help him through marital difficulties. None of his wives is named in the Qur'an, though their situation is clearly described. The instructions, in each case, are tailored to Muhammad's situation, but the Lord's rulings have juridical implications—for sumptuary laws, for divorce as a punishment, for incest legislation, and for scandal prosecution.

1. *Sumptuary Laws.* One or more of Muhammad's wives wanted to have more finery as a sign of their status, though Muhammad lived modestly and counseled others to do so. God tells the Prophet to divorce any wives who do not wish to live by his standards:

> Prophet, say to your wives, "If your desire is for the present life and its finery, then come, I will make provision for you and release you with kindness, but if you desire God, His Messenger, and the Final Home, then remember that God has prepared great rewards for those of you who do good." (33.28)

"Release with kindness" was a formula for divorce, which had many uses at the time and which should be reached as amicably as possible (4.128).

2. *Divorce as Punishment.* Divorce was easily obtained by men, and Allah advises it as a method of control when Muhammad's wives collaborate to protest his treatment of them. When one wife questioned an action by the Prophet—the commentators say it was for unequal sexual favors (SQ 1389)—Muhammad tested whether she would tell another wife, stirring up discontent among "collaborators." Then he confronted the one he had pledged to silence. The

offender is informed that she and the one she told can easily be traded for a "better" wife.

> The Prophet told something in confidence to one of his wives. When she disclosed it [to another wife] and God made this known to him, he confirmed part of it, and said nothing about the rest. When he confronted her with what she had done, she asked, "Who told you about this?" and he replied, "The All Knowing, the All Aware told me." If both of you [wives] repent to God—for your hearts have deviated—[all will be well]; if you collaborate against him, [be warned that] God will aid him, as will Gabriel and all righteous believers, and the angels too will back him. His Lord may well replace you with better wives if the Prophet decides to divorce you: wives who are devoted to God, true believers, devout, who turn to Him in repentance and worship Him, given to fasting, whether previously married or virgins. (66.3–5)

3. *Incest Law.* Muhammad arranged a marriage between his adopted son, Zayd, and a woman named Zayda. But Zayda wanted to marry Muhammad, and her husband agreed to let her go. Muhammad refused her offer, fearing that the populace would consider it incestuous for him to marry his son's wife. Allah assures him that incest law does not treat an adopted son as a natural son, and tells him to obey his God-prompted heart, not the populace (SQ 1030–31).

> When you [Prophet] said to the man who had been favoured by God and by you, "Keep your wife and be mindful of God," you hid in your heart what God would later reveal: you were afraid of people, but it is more fitting that you fear God. When Zayd no longer wanted her, We gave her to you

in marriage so that there might be no fault in believers marrying the wives of their adopted sons after they no longer wanted them. God's command must be carried out: the Prophet is not at fault for what God has ordained for him. This was God's practice with those who went before [*that is, the polygynous prophets of the Old Testament*]—God's command must be fulfilled—[and with all] those who deliver God's messages and fear only Him and no other: God's reckoning is enough. Muhammad is not the father of any one of you men [*that is, of Zayd*]; he is God's Messenger and the seal of the prophets: God knows everything. (33.37–40)

4. *Scandal Prosecution.* In this case, unlike the first three, Muhammad's own situation is more assumed than described in the Qur'an itself, but it is plausibly explained in the early ahadith as applying to the story of A'ishah, reputedly the most bright and beautiful of his wives (and therefore the most likely to be resented by other wives, and to be subject to their insinuations).[3] A group is darkly accused of bringing "the false accusation"—presumably against A'ishah—and this is the occasion for setting strict rules for scandal prosecution. According to the traditions, A'ishah twice left a caravan to search for a lost necklace. She stayed out overnight, was searched for and found, and was then accused of committing adultery with the one who found her. Though there are many detailed versions of this story in the ahadith, the Qur'an just tells of its consequences for her accusers (SQ 870–71).

As for those who accuse chaste women of fornication, and then fail to provide four witnesses, strike them eighty times, and reject their testimony ever afterwards; they are the lawbreakers, except for those who repent later and make amends— God is most forgiving and merciful. . . . It was a group from among you who brought the false accusation—do not consider it a bad thing for you [people]; it was a good thing—and every one of them will be charged with the sin he has earned. He who took the greatest part in it will have a painful torment. When you heard the lie, why did believing men and women not think well of their own people and declare, "This is obviously a lie?" And why did the accusers not bring four witnesses to it? If they cannot produce such witnesses, they are the liars in God's eyes. If it were not for God's bounty and mercy towards you in this world and the next, you would already have been afflicted by terrible suffering for indulging in such talk. When you took it up with your tongues, and spoke with your mouths things you did not know [to be true], you thought it was trivial but to God it was very serious. When you heard the lie, why did you not say, "We should not repeat this—God forbid!—It is a monstrous slander"? God warns you never to do anything like this again, if you are true believers. God makes His messages clear to you: God is all knowing, all wise. A painful torment waits in this world and the next for those who like indecency to spread among the believers: God knows and you do not. (24.4, 11–19)

Why does the text say that the false accusation was not "a bad thing for you"? That depends on who the "you" are. Caner Dagli, in *The Study Quran* (870–71), says there are three possible audiences. One could be the community of believers, which was in a turmoil of suspicion and accusation, which is now resolved. Or it might be the narrower group of believers responsible for carrying out the law—they now have a definitive procedure for handling scandal prosecutions. It might even be the false accusers themselves—their evil careers have been arrested, so they may become virtuous members of the community (perhaps after getting eighty lashes).

Once again, this kind of inhibition on baseless gossip makes greatest sense in terms of Muhammad's harem, where the fostering of accusation, suspicion, and solidarity against their husband could unravel a whole community of co-wives. The politics of the harem are not to be conceived of as a tyranny. The women are not the unquestioning slaves of a sultan. They are wives, which means they have entered marriage voluntarily, receiving the substantial bride-wealth all wives are given by their husbands. They are free to divorce the husband. And if they do not want to be divorced by him, they have various bargaining chips they can play—a fact that makes Allah say that the husbands should exercise authority fairly and gently.

> If a wife fears high-handedness or alienation from her hus-
> band, neither of them will be blamed if they come to a peace-
> ful settlement, for peace is best. Although human souls are
> prone to selfishness, if you do good and are mindful of God,
> He is well aware of all that you do. You will never be able to
> treat your wives with equal fairness, however much you may
> desire to do so, but do not ignore one wife altogether, leaving
> her suspended [between marriage and divorce]. (4.128–29)

Haleem's addition to the text, about suspension over whether to get a divorce, may be true in the long run. But the more imme-
diate thing needed for resolution is the suspension of the order of rotation among the wives' special days. We know such an order exists, since Allah says that Muhammad does not have to follow it invariably (though he should not entirely neglect one wife).

> You may make any of [your women] wait and receive any of
> them as you wish, but you will not be at fault if you invite one
> whose turn you have previously set aside: this way it is more

likely that they will be satisfied and will not be distressed and will be content with what you have given them. (33.51)

This permission to vary the routine of attention among wives gives, I believe, a better explanation to a contested verse than the one almost universally accepted.

Your wives are [like] your fields, so go into your fields whichever way you like, and send [something good] ahead for yourselves. (2.223)

Haleem assumes that "go into your fields" means to plow them. This is usually taken as a husband's right to have sex in whatever way he wants, man on top or woman on top, man in front of woman, or man behind, or both on their sides—against any possible objections from the woman (SQ 98). But how many ways are there to plow a field—circular, or straight from the same end, or boustrophedon? And which of these could be considered the field's top or bottom, front or back? Agrarian images are common in the New Testament but not in the Qur'an. What special knowledge of ways to plow is this surah assuming?

What Haleem translates with "*go into*" and "*whichever way* you like" is given in *The Study Quran:* "Your women are a tilth to you, so *go unto* your tilth *as* you will." Pickthall (1930) accords with SQ: "*go to* your tilth *as* ye will." But Ali (1934) expands that conjunction "as" even more than Haleem does: "approach your tilth *when or how* ye will." Shakir (1999) may be getting closer to what seems to me the right interpretation: "*go into* your tilth *when* you like." Dawood, who can be eccentric, somehow turns the conjunction "as" into "whence," as in point of origin: "Go then into your fields whence you please."[4]

We don't have in the Qur'an (as opposed to the ahadith) any

discussion of sexual positions. It makes no sense to find it in this one place, when we do have references to the care and timing of attention to different wives. What is the real parallel with care of fields? It is the attentions apportioned to different fields and their crops. The farmer must rotate his crops as the Muslim must vary his attentions and favors, including sexual attentions among his wives.

This reading also gives a better sense to the rest of the verse. That reads in SQ: "So go unto your tilth as you will, *but send forth for your souls.*"

Send what, we may ask, and how is the soul benefited by the sending? SQ glosses: "Send forth means to perform good deeds that will benefit one in the Hereafter." Different sexual positions are unlikely to have heavenly rewards, which means Haleem has to make a different (but no less obscure) translation of the verse's end words: "Go into your fields whichever way you like, and send [something good] ahead for yourselves." Pickthall's translation is close to SQ: "but do some good act for your souls beforehand." Shakir, too, is enigmatic: "and do good beforehand for yourselves." If the image is of the husband distributing his care equitably, he would bring peace to his home if he declared that policy, even when it is the normal turn for a different woman.

I am reminded, perhaps trivially, of a time in the early 1960s when I spent a day with the Catholic bishop (later cardinal) John Wright of Pittsburgh to write an article on him. In the course of a long day, we were driven in his chauffeured limousine to one of his favorite charities, a home for unwed mothers (a project common then). I thought of the home as his chaste harem. When we entered, the women were glad to see him. He was familiar with each one's story—some abandoned with their children, some pregnant, some with babies. Before he went in, he had the chauffeur open the trunk of his limousine, where he had a large collection of dolls, larger and more realistic than Barbie dolls, which the manufacturer gave to him for charity uses. He gave carefully selected dolls to the children inside or to the pregnant women as gifts for the baby when born. These were just some of the presents, the comforting words, the career advice, he was known for devoting to them. He had dinner with the women almost once a week, and his thoughtfulness made me think of the care a husband would need to manifest in order to keep peace among the co-wives in a plural marriage.

This passage of the Qur'an prompts another memory. When Martin Marty and Scott Appleby were doing the research that went into their lengthy study of religious fundamentalisms around the world, they invited me to sit in on some of their interviews with different kinds of fundamentalists. One whose interview I attended was with a woman who was part of a dissident Mormon sect that observed the religion's original polygyny. She was a successful lawyer, who told us how she considered her marriage liberating. She had her regular night to be with her husband, and she was free the rest of the time to pursue her career. She said that, on her night, she and her husband had sex if they wanted to, but often just talked about their multiple interests and their separate careers. This is a far cry from Muhammad's marriages, of course, but it made me think of the ways care must be sorted out in any plural marriage. This Mormon woman had entered into her marriage voluntarily and with certain promises from the outset. That was also true of polygynous marriages in the Qur'an. It may seem odd to us, but there were women's rights even in those marriages, including the right to withdraw from the marriage. That should be taken up next.

NOTES

1. Jonathan A. C. Brown, *Muhammad: A Very Short Introduction* (Oxford University Press, 2011), pp. 43, 49–53, 75–78.
2. Ibid., p. 76.

3. A'ishah is reported to have been nine when Muhammad married her, which has led to a great deal of criticism of the Prophet, but early marriages were common until recently, and no one knows when this one was consummated. As Jonathan Brown writes: "Interestingly, no critic of Muhammad, from his fiercest opponents in the Quraysh to medieval Christian clerics, objected to his marriage to so young a wife until the modern period. This is noteworthy, since there has certainly never been a shortage of detractors seeking chinks in the armour of Muhammad's character to exploit" (ibid., p. 77).

4. Hafiz Abdullah Yusuf Ali, Mohammed Marmaduke Pickthall, Muhammad Habib Shakir, *Three Translations of the Koran (Al-Qur'an) Side by Side* (Flying Chipmunk Publishing, 2009), p. 31. N. J. Dawood, *The Koran* (Penguin Books, 2014), p. 23.

CHAPTER 12

Women: Fighting Back

Torah, Gospel, and Qur'an are all patriarchal, and therefore misogynist—as were the societies in which they took shape. But misogynism is not *all* that all of them are. In all three of them there are traces of dignity and worth intended by the Creator when he made women. The task for feminists is to identify, investigate, and develop these traces.

That is not an easy task, for any of the three traditions. Belief in women's inferiority is a long and disheartening part of each tradition's story. For almost all of Jewish history, no woman could become a rabbi. For almost all of Christian history, no woman could become a priest. For almost all of Muslim history, no woman could become a prophet (though scores of men did) or an imam (thousands of men did). This is not surprising, given the views that were considered authoritative, and the grounds for those views:

Aristotle said that woman is a botched man (*arrēn pepērōmanon*).[1]

Thomas Aquinas said that woman is an accidental man (*mas occasionatus*).[2]

The Qur'an says that woman is half a man—at least for certain transactions. Like inheriting:

Concerning your children, God commands you that a son should have the equivalent share of two daughters. (4.11)

Or for witnessing contracts:

Call in two men as witnesses. If two men are not there, then call one man and two women out of those you approve as witnesses, so that if one of the two women should forget the other can remind her. (2.282)

Some defenders of the Qur'an try to soften the message of these passages:

On *inheriting*, they argue that any inheritance at all is an advance for women, since it had earlier been thought that those unable to fight wars or be political leaders were not contributors to society important enough to have or manage property. (SQ 193)

On *witnessing*, they say the contracts take some expertise, so women are not essentially inferior if they merely lack that expertise (SQ 123). In a culture where women were less literate than men (Muhammad, after all, was illiterate himself), that may be another reason why they would not be able to acquire the necessary expertise. But it was misogynism that denied them the chance to read in the first place. There is no denying that in early Islam women were "second-class citizens"—or they would have been if the concept of citizen had existed at the time. On the worth of women, the Torah and the Gospel cannot boast more enlightenment than the Qur'an.

Consider again the "hitting verse" mentioned in the last chapter. We cannot imagine the Qur'an telling a wife under what conditions she should punch her husband. This "hitting verse" is to women what the "sword verse" (9.5) is to war. Muslims rightly show great discomfort at these words. In Haleem's sixteen-page chapter on marriage in the Qur'an, ten are spent trying to ameliorate what this one verse says.[3] His effort gets rather desperate:

> All Muslim exegetes agree that the husband is not allowed to beat his wife severely, since the Prophet said "without severity." In fact, most say that it has to be so light as to be with something like a tooth stick/toothbrush.[4]

I think a modern Muslim who threatened his wife with a toothbrush might become guilty of killing her—with laughter.

Maria Massi Dakake, in *The Study Quran,* devotes to the hitting verse five dense columns of commentary and three more pages of an appended essay (SQ 206–8, 1794–96). According to Dakake, "to *strike* here refers only to a moderate and non-injurious form of physical force," with no "license to commit physical violence or inflict bodily harm," and "strictly for the purpose of altering the wife's behavior" (SQ 208). "Furthermore, some contemporary Muslim scholars and authorities have argued that the Arabic word usually translated 'hit' or 'strike' should be interpreted differently and that it perhaps means simply to go away from one's wife" (SQ 1796). This is the exegetical method of Humpty Dumpty: "When I use a word, it means just what I choose it to mean."

The American Muslim Amina Wadud and the Pakistani Islam scholar Asma Barlas argue that in 4.34 *daraba* can mean "to strike," "to set an example," and "to separate," and is not the same as *darraba,* which means "to strike repeatedly." So the verse is *opposed* to a previous culture's wife beating.[5]

The prospects for women's rights in the Qur'an seem very dark—but they are partly brightened when we discover that a wife has a cure for punches: she can just leave, and take her property with her. Women, who freely marry in the first place, can divorce their husbands. If, on the other hand, she might want to stay married (even after being punched), she can use her property as a bargaining chip for better treatment or for sullen acceptance.

> If a wife fears high-handedness or alienation from her husband, neither of them will be blamed if they come to a peaceful settlement, for peace is best. (4.128)

Dakake glosses this verse in *The Study Quran:*

> According to most commentators [on 4.128], this means agreeing to give her husband part of her bridal payment or other property or forfeiting some of her rights as a wife (e.g., to conjugal relations or financial maintenance) in order to remain married to her husband and avoid desertion or divorce. Because of the possibility of polygamy in Islam, this may mean agreeing to allow her husband to spend more time or money on another (perhaps younger or more desirable) co-wife. (SQ 250)

This is a language of power relations and their negotiation—not something we expect or find in either the Old Testament or the New Testament. In fact, the treatment of women in the Qur'an, even after we admit the general patriarchal setting, offers better grounds for feminism than are supplied in the other sacred writings. In the Old Testament, Satan first deceives Eve, as the weaker partner. In the Qur'an both husband and wife are tempted equally and fall equally, and they are henceforth punished equally for sins like adultery (one hundred lashes for either one regardless of gender) and they are rewarded equally for their virtue:

For men and women who are devoted to God—believing
men and women, obedient men and women, truthful men and
women, steadfast men and women, humble men and women,
charitable men and women, fasting men and women, chaste
men and women, men and women who remember God often—
God has prepared forgiveness and a rich reward. (33.35)

In the Old Testament, Eve is a later and lesser creation. God
creates Adam directly from primal earth, but Eve is made from
Adam's rib. Thomas Aquinas tells us why. Adam needed a companion (Gn 2.20) but male companionship is superior to that of a
woman—the only new thing she can offer is her ability to bear
man's heirs.[6]

Contrast that with the creation of Adam's wife in the Qur'an.
She is a later but not a lesser creation. She is made not from Adam
but from the same stuff as Adam. And the only reason she is later
is to make sure that all humans come from one point of origin,
making humans all equally sons or daughters of God.

People, be mindful of our Lord, who created you from a single soul, and from it created its mate, and from the pair of
them spread countless men and women far and wide. (4.1)[7]

Elsewhere it is said that Adam and his wife originated from water
(21.30, 24.45), from dust (30.20), from clay (7.12), from a drop of fluid
(36.77). Obviously the materials used are less important than the uni-
tary origin of the whole race. The solidarity of the human race reflects
the oneness of God—the primary doctrine of Islam (SQ 189).

One aspect of the Qur'an is largely taken to show the inferiority
of women—their sequestration or veiling. That is such an ingrained
perception that I put it off till the next chapter for separate treatment.

Veiling is only indirectly mentioned in the Qur'an. But a more practical source of female power is constantly talked of in the Qur'an—the money given a woman in marriage. This can easily be misconceived in its purpose and effect. It can look at first like the purchase of a bride. But if she were being sold, the money would go to her seller (her father or guardian). But no, the money goes directly to her, and she retains it even in the marriage, and even after divorce. She can waive her right to it, but it cannot be forced from her.

This has been called, misleadingly, a kind of reverse dowry. The familiar dowry known from European history was paid by the bride's father to the family of the groom. The quandary of a man with more daughters than he could afford to marry into socially desirable families led to the shunting of "extra" daughters into convents—just as primogeniture led to the shunting of "extra" sons into the church or into the military services.[8] In this case, the bride was a medium of exchange—at a cost to her family. In Qur'anic marriage, the cost was to the groom's family, but it did not pass through to her family. It stopped with her. In a commercial society like that of Muhammad, this gave the wife a stable asset. Dakake rightly says of this extraordinary provision:

> Perhaps the most revolutionary social principle introduced by the Quran was the notion of women's right to property—that is, the right, upon legal maturity, to own and to dispose of property independently of either their husbands or their male relatives. The Quran established the women's right to property through the institutions of both marital dowry and inheritance. The Quran specifies in numerous places that a man must pay his wife a mandatory bridal gift upon the contraction of their marriage and that this must be a free gift that cannot be alienated from her against her will (4.4); nor can it be taken from her after a divorce or after she has been

widowed, except in cases where she has criminally violated
her marital obligations through adultery (4.19).

Dakake's language is a bit loose here. The money paid is not a
dowry in any of the senses we are familiar with, and it is not, strictly
speaking, a gift—something that can be offered or omitted at the
will of the giver. It is the marriage contract itself. So true is this that
a Muslim man can only marry the believing divorced wife of a pagan
husband by returning the marriage payment given by the pagan.
This is the only bride-gift that can be taken away from a law-abiding
woman. Though Haleem, the translation I use for uniformity, translates this item as "bride-gift," *The Study Quran* gets closer to the truth
with its term, "bridewealth," something she can dispose of entirely
on her own. The more accurate word would be "bride-right." The
idea of the bride's right is reflected in two of the terms used for it in
the Qur'an—*suduqat* (4.4) and *farridah* (2.236), which both mean
"obligation." The third term, *ujur* (4.24), "wages," also refers to what
the woman can claim as a right.[9]

A marriage can be completed only on sexual consummation.
But that is true of marriage in our modern sense, too. Our marriage
ceremony constitutes the legal state of marriage—which may be
broken off if there is no sexual consummation, but only by another
legal procedure (divorce). In the modern case, the husband is not
automatically liable for support (though that may be negotiated).
In the Qur'an, the wife gets to keep half of the bride-right, even
though there was no consummation. She is encouraged to waive the
right—but so is the husband (that is, he is encouraged to let go the
whole bride-right) (SQ 104):

If you divorce wives before consummating the marriage but
after fixing a bride-gift for them, then give them half of what
you had previously fixed, unless they waive [their right], or

unless the one who holds the marriage tie [*i.e., the payer of the bride-right, the husband*] waives [his right]. Waiving [your right] is nearer to godliness, so do not forget to be generous towards one another: God sees what you do. (2.237)

Even if the amount of the bride-right has not been agreed upon during negotiation for a marriage, the husband-to-be is still bound to support the woman he began the bargaining with:

There is no obligation on you if you divorce women when you have not consummated the marriage or fixed a bride-gift for them, but make fair provision for them, the rich according to his means and the poor according to his—this is a duty for those who do good. (2.236)

Some men might think twice about divorce when they realize that if she goes, her bride-right goes with her:

If you wish to replace one wife with another, do not take back any of her bride-gift, even if you have given her a great amount of gold. How could you take it when this is unjust and a blatant sin? How could you take it when you have lain with each other and they have taken a solemn pledge from you? (4.20–21)

The bride-right is something sacrosanct. It cannot be revoked or tampered with—though it can be used as a family asset with her permission. That is another motive for the husband to foster a respectful relationship.

If you wish to enjoy women [through marriage], give them their bride-gift—this is obligatory—though if you should choose mutually, after fulfilling this obligation, to do otherwise [with the bride-gift], you will not be blamed: God is all knowing and all wise. (4.24)

If a man cannot afford the bride-right a free woman demands, he can marry a believing slave woman—belief in the One God makes them all His children—but he must still pay the bride-right (just a lesser one to the slave).

If any of you does not have the means to marry a believing free woman, then marry a believing slave—God knows best [the depth of] your faith: you [*as believers*] are [all] part of the same family—so marry them with their people's consent and their proper bride-gifts, [making them] married women, not adulteresses or lovers. (4.25)

Though a Muslim could have sexual intercourse with pagan slaves he had won, bought, or captured (4.24, 23.6), he could not do so with believers in the One God (including Jews and Christians). If he desired them, he must marry them:

This [*marriage with a believing slave*] is for those of you who fear that you will sin; it is better for you to practise self-restraint. (4.25)

This is remarkably like Paul's injunction:

I tell the unmarried or the widowed it is a goal to remain single, as I do. But if they lack self-discipline, they must marry, since it is better to be married than to be inflamed. (1 Cor 7.8–9)

We have seen earlier that marriage with Jews or Christians was allowed by Allah:

Today all good things have been made lawful for you. The food of the People of the Book [*Jews*] is lawful for you as your food is lawful for them. So are chaste, believing, women as well as chaste women of the people who were given the Scripture [*Christians*] before you, as long as you have given them their bride-gifts and married them, not taken them as lovers or secret mistresses. (5.5)

The fact that there can be multiple wives does not mean that the Qur'an takes marriage lightly. It orders believers to treasure their spouses. God considers the bestowal of spouses one of his special blessings to mankind:

Another of His signs is that He created spouses from among yourselves for you to live with in tranquillity; He ordained love and kindness between you. (30.21)

The spouses are like each other's garment—so much so that Allah made an exception for them to have intercourse even during the Fast (2.187). The spousal bond is sacred still, and highly honored, even in heaven (13.23, 25.74–76, 52.20). This is one point where the Qur'an and the New Testament part company. When a Sadducee brings up levirate marriages to Jesus (men marrying their brother's widow) and asks which man will be her husband in heaven, Jesus answers:

Jesus said in answer to them, "You are wide of the mark, knowing neither Scripture nor God's way. At the Resurrection, there are no husbands and wives. In heaven, they are like angels." (Mt 22.30)

The Qur'an makes marriage eternal, while in Matthew's Gospel its tie is merely temporal. The Qur'an is therefore protective of marriage, discouraging impulsive divorce by imposing waiting periods and proposing mediation to bring disaffected partners back together. After a motion to divorce, there must be a pause to assure that there is not a child in gestation to be considered. Since women as well as men can initiate a divorce, the men must wait four months before completing the divorce; women must wait to complete three menstrual cycles during which God may bring the partners to a renewed appreciation of each other.

> For those who swear that they will not approach their wives, there shall be a waiting period of four months: if they go back, remember that God will be most forgiving and merciful, but if they are determined to divorce, remember that God hears and knows all. Divorced women must wait for three monthly periods before remarrying, and if they really believe in God and the Last Day, it is not lawful for them to conceal what God has created in their wombs: their husbands would do better to take them back during this period, provided they wish to put things right. [Divorced] women have [rights] similar to their obligations, according to what is fair, and [ex-]husbands have a degree [of right] over them: [both should remember that] God is almighty and wise. (2.226–28)

The spouses' care and respect for each other should prevail, even in a difficult time, along with a hope that a full break will be put off long enough to make it no longer necessary.

> Prophet, when any of you intend to divorce women, do so at a time when their prescribed waiting period can properly start, and calculate the period carefully: be mindful of God, your Lord. Do not make them leave their homes—nor should they themselves leave—unless they commit a flagrant indecency.

These are the limits set by God—those who overstep God's limits wrong their own souls—for you cannot know what new situation God may perhaps bring about.

When they have completed their appointed term, either keep them honourably, or part with them honourably. Call two just witnesses from your people and establish witness for the sake of God. Anyone who believes in God and the Last Day should heed this: God will find a way out for those who are mindful of Him, and will provide for them from an unexpected source; God will be enough for those who put their trust in Him. God achieves His purpose; God has set a due measure for everything.

If you are in doubt, the period of waiting will be three months for those women who have ceased menstruating and for those who have not [yet] menstruated; the waiting period of those who are pregnant will be until they deliver their burden: God makes things easy for those who are mindful of Him. This is God's command, which He has sent down to you. God will wipe out the sinful deeds and increase the rewards of anyone who is mindful of Him.

House the wives you are divorcing according to your means, wherever you house yourselves, and do not harass them so as to make their lives difficult. If they are pregnant, maintain them until they are delivered of their burdens; if they suckle your infants, pay them for it. Consult together in a good way—if you make difficulties for one another, another woman may suckle the child for the father—and let the wealthy man spend according to his wealth. But let him whose provision is restricted spend according to what God has given him: God does not burden any soul with more than He has given it—after hardship, God will bring ease. (65.1–7)

Saving a marriage by counseling is another important theme of the Qur'an:

If you [believers] fear that a couple may break up, appoint one arbiter from his family and one from hers. Then, if the couple want to put things right, God will bring about a reconciliation between them: He is all knowing, all aware. (4.35)

Even when a marriage has been ended by divorce, it may still be saved:

Divorce can happen twice, and [each time] wives either be kept on in an acceptable manner or released in a good way. It is not lawful for you to take back anything [*of the bride-right*] that you have given [your wives], except where both fear that they cannot maintain [the marriage within] the bounds set by God: if you [arbiters] suspect that the couple may not be able to do this, then there will be no blame on either of them if the woman opts to give something [*from her bride-right*] for her release. . . . If a husband re-divorces his wife after the second divorce, she will not be lawful for him until she has taken another husband; if that one divorces her, there will be no blame if she and the first husband return to one another, provided they feel they can keep within the bounds set by God. (2.229–30)

Women are not merely passive objects of men's management but agents with negotiable assets. In a commercial society these were not a negligible consideration. Even in mid-twentieth-century America, a woman was often not able to open a bank account or make a major purchase without her husband's or guardian's approval. Women of the Qur'an were better off in that respect.

In other words, the inhabitants of a harem were not slaves, as in some presentations of the *Arabian Nights*. They were reminded of their status by the presence of actual slave women who did the "women's work" of housekeeping (harem keeping). Poor white women in our antebellum South were not as discontented with their lot as they might have been did they not feel and express superiority to their "Negro" slaves. That is a poor way to achieve dignity; but it was one of several better ways available to women in the original Muslim world.

Of course many practices and judgments, wrought by history's uneven development and distortions, would make women far more vulnerable than they had been in the Qur'an. But, as Leila Ahmed writes of what she calls Establishment Islam:

Only within this politically powerful version of Islam (and in its reflection in Western Orientalist literature)—a version with no greater claim to being regarded as the only possible interpretation of Islam than Papal Christianity has to being regarded as the only possible interpretation of Christianity— is women's position immutably fixed as subordinate.[10]

The work of Muslim feminists has been to go back to what began in the Qur'an and develop it on an alternate path from that taken in the imperialist days of Islam. It is the same work that Christian feminists have been engaged in: to see the initial gains for women made in the Gospels and in the Epistles of Paul before the patriarchism of the medieval church erased those beginnings.

NOTES

1. Aristotle, *Animal Breeding* (*Peri Zōōn Geneseōs*) 737a28. "The male should be set apart from the female, since the former is better and more godlike in the

way it imparts activity to what is generated. The female supplies matter [for male form]." Ibid. 732a7-9.

2. Thomas Aquinas, *Summa Theologica* I q92 a1 ad 1: "The female is an accidental male, since the active male seed intends to produce a perfect image of itself; but if a female results, it is because there was a lessened effect in the active seed, or because there was some inadequacy in the matter, or because of some interference by an external cause, like the humidity of the south wind."

3. Muhammad Abdel Haleem, *Understanding the Qur'an: Themes and Style* (I. B. Tauris, 1999), pp. 48–57.

4. Ibid., pp. 55–56.

5. Quoted in Asma Barlas, "Women's Readings of the Qur'an," in Jane Dammen McAuliffe, *The Cambridge Companion to the Qur'an* (Cambridge University Press, 2006), pp. 263–64.

6. Thomas Aquinas, *Summa Theologica* I q92 resp: "Man can be more thoroughly accompanied by another man in other activities, but not in the begetting of other humans."

7. See restatements at 6.98, 7.189, 31.28, 39.6.

8. Mary Laven, *Virgins of Venice: Broken Vows and Cloistered Lives in the Renaissance Convent* (Viking, 2003), pp. 34–38.

9. For reasons, I suppose, of legal fixity, the term for bride-right in Islamic law, *mahr*, is not in the Qur'an itself, though the concept is the same in all these usages.

10. Leila Ahmed, *Women and Gender in Islam* (Yale University Press, 1992), p. 239.

CHAPTER 13

Women: The Veil

That so much energy has been expended by Muslim men and then Muslim women to remove the veil and by others to affirm or restore it is frustrating and ludicrous.

—LEILA AHMED[1]

Those are words Professor Ahmed, of the Harvard Divinity School, wrote in 1992. But she then spent most of the last four chapters of her book on the "frustrating and ludicrous" subject of the Muslim women's veil—and she was right to do it. It is a subject that has been at the center of many debates over the last two centuries. Even Muslim feminists are divided on the issue, some rushing to tear off Muslim women's veils, while others rush to put them back on. That is why I see so many students wearing hijabs on American campuses. Some, like Larycia Hawkins at Wheaton College, are not themselves Muslims, but are voicing a sisterly respect for those who are. How did what many thought a sign of female degradation become, for others, a badge of Muslim feminism?

Some people might be surprised to hear there is such a thing as a Muslim feminist. In fact, there are many of them.[2] Some even wear the hijab—as a symbol of their feminism, though many think it stands for everything feminists must oppose. For them, removing the veil is a way of giving in to Western colonialism. I mentioned in chapter 2 the way anti-colonial movements after World War II sparked a fundamentalist resistance on the part of local cultures. Michael Walzer noted that "modernizers" in Israel, Algeria, and India were considered sellouts when they tried to introduce Western concepts like the broad franchise, secularism, and women's rights. The secularists of the late-twentieth century triggered the kind of religious backlash studied in Martin Marty's Fundamentalism Project.

But if the cultural recrudescence Marty studied was a late-twentieth-century phenomenon, Leila Ahmed finds a similar dynamic at play in an early-twentieth-century development. The secular "protectorates" established in the Middle East and North Africa provoked some modern Muslim women to defend their traditional culture, including (for some of them) the veil.[3] They were reacting against European overseers like Evelyn Baring, the Earl of Cromer, who ruled Egypt from the time (1882) when England replaced France as the guardian of the Suez Canal. For the next twenty-five years Cromer was what Edward Said called "the paramount consul-general in England's empire."[4]

Cromer ruled by his self-proclaimed skill at managing "the Oriental mind"—which could be made to work only when it recognized the superior culture of its British overseers.[5] He wanted to show the empire's benevolent rule of it subjects. For him, the muffling of women just proved that they had been victims of the Oriental mind. The women could join the modern world by rejecting their men's ideas. This meant, Ahmed claims, that women could advance under British protection only by the ruthless criticism of their own family and culture: they were recruited into a new subservience in order to escape subservience. This is what Ahmed calls "internalized colonization," whereby the woman takes off the veil as a way of despising her own people. It was a clever way to advance empire as a form of *subjected* liberation.

[This] captured the language of feminism and redirected it, in the service of colonialism, toward Other men and the cultures of Other men. It was here and in the combining of the languages of colonialism and feminism that the fusion between the issues of women and culture was created. More exactly, what was created was the fusion between the issues of women, their oppression, and the cultures of Other men. The idea that Other men, men in colonized societies or societies beyond the borders of the civilized West, oppressed women was to be used, in the rhetoric of colonialism, to render morally justifiable its project of undermining or eradicating the cultures of colonized peoples.[6]

Ahmed notes the irony—Lord Cromer, who claimed to be freeing Muslim women in Egypt, opposed letting English women get the vote in his own country. This was part of a larger pattern:

The Victorian colonial paternalistic establishment appropriated the language of feminism in the service of its assault on the religions and cultures of Other men, and in particular on Islam, in order to give an aura of moral justification to that assault at the very same time as it combated feminism within its own society. . . . This champion [Cromer] of the unveiling of Egyptian women was, in England, a founding member and sometime president of the Men's League for Opposing Women's Suffrage. Feminism on the home front and feminism directed against white men was to be resisted and suppressed; but taken abroad and directed against the cultures of colonized people, it could be promoted in ways that admirably served and furthered the project of the dominance of the white man.[7]

Cromer was able to use foreign-trained Muslims in the British civil service to spread his message, which was essentially "Here come the foreigners to rescue our women." Ahmed is scathing about one especially famous person, Qasim Amin, the founder of Cairo University, who wrote *The Liberation of Women* in 1899. This gave him an early reputation as a friend to the pioneer feminists. But Ahmed finds that Amin was spreading the gospel according to Cromer.

The ideas to which Cromer and the [Christian] missionaries gave expression formed the basis of Amin's book. The rationale in which Amin, a French-educated upper-middle-class lawyer, grounded his call for changing the position of women and for abolishing the veil was essentially the same as theirs.[8]

Walzer found that a prime cause for renewed fundamentalism was the way colonized people's countrymen introduced Western ideas to correct their evil ways. What was true of Nehru in India and Fanon in Algeria after World War II was also true of Amin after World War I. The cry of these people—"Here comes the West to rescue our women"—was raised again after 9/11. Two months after that atrocity, while President Bush was assembling the troops to invade Afghanistan, his wife, Laura, became the first woman to present solo the president's traditional Saturday radio broadcast. She said that the war against terrorism was "a fight for the rights and dignity of women," because of which "the people of Afghanistan, especially women, are rejoicing."[9] This was her version of what the men around Bush were claiming—that our soldiers would have flowers thrown at them by those they had "liberated." Mrs. Bush was right to oppose the suppression of women in Afghanistan, but presenting that as a rationale for invasion in a "war on terror" sounded far different in the country being invaded than it did in the White House—just as her husband's use of the word "crusade" grated in the Middle East.

Leila Ahmed, reacting against the opportunistic feminism of Western invaders, argues for a feminism that retains the women's veil. Her reasons are mainly secular—to protect the history of the endemic cultures, to remain in solidarity with one's countrywomen who are veiled, to ease the exchanges with Western feminists (like Larycia Hawkins), to protect the status of Muslim women "out in the world," even to give a more economical way of clothing.

> These practical advantages partially explain why university and professional women in particular adopt Islamic dress— women who daily venture onto coeducational campuses and into sexually integrated work places on crowded public transport in cities in which, given the strong rural origin of much of the population, sexually integrated social space is still an alien, uncomfortable social reality for both women and men. Thus the ritual invocation through dress of the notion of segregation places the integrated reality in a framework that defuses it of stress and impropriety. At the same time it declares women's presence in public space to be in no way a challenge to or a violation of the Islamic sociocultural ethic.[10]

Thus far the secular argument. But what does the Qur'an say about veiling women? Actually, not much. The aya that has been called "the veiling verse" (SQ 1035) has nothing to do with women's clothing. It is as misunderstood as is the "sword verse" or the "hitting verse" considered earlier. It comes in a section of Surah 33 that is devoted to what might be called the traffic laws of the Prophet's home (33.49–58). This discusses the special treatment of Muhammad's wives, their qualifications, their number, their brideright (given or waived), their protection from divorce or remarriage, their treatment by turns. All this section concerns the Prophet's special status and that of his wives. Just as he is the intimate father of believers, his wives are their honorary mothers (33.55). There are no general rules here for the treatment of ordinary women.

> This is only for you [Prophet] and not the rest of the believers. We know exactly what We have made obligatory for them concerning their wives and slave-girls—so you should not be blamed [*for being different*]: God is most forgiving, most merciful. (33.50)

The access and the etiquette of visiting the Prophet in his busy home are being decreed. In that context, here comes the "veiling verse":

> When you ask his wives for something, do so from behind a screen: this is purer both for your hearts and for theirs. (33.53)

What Haleem translates as "screen" is "veil" in the SQ. It says nothing about how the wives should be clothed, and it does not say that only men have to speak through the screen. This is the way petitions ("when you ask for something") are submitted. It is an orderly procedure, one that spares the wives from possibly embarrassing personal confrontations. Which wife, for instance, is answering the man or woman on the other side of the screen—along with any tensions between the wives in the response—these matters are kept subordinate to the substance of the petitions. The wives are kept "in cloister," as it were—a succeeding verse gives the rules by which others, mainly relatives and slave women, can enter and talk in the cloisters (33.55). None of this is different from the procedures around some nuns of my youth.

Well, if the veiling verse has nothing to do with veils worn by women, what verses do address that? There are two.

Prophet, tell your wives, your daughters, and women believers to make their outer garments hang low over them, so as to be recognized and not insulted: God is most forgiving, most merciful. (33.59)

This verse gives the reason for modesty of dress—"be recognized." Recognized as what? The SQ (1038) says that this dress distinguishes free women from slaves. It may also distinguish Muslim women from pagans or prostitutes. It could mean any or all of these. But the common element in all these hypotheses is that the distinction elevates the women. It does not, as many people think, demean them. Some might think that Amish dress is forced on men or women, though they clearly think it is a badge of honor. The same could be said of other religious signs worn with pride— the Jews' yarmulkes or sheitels, Roman collars or cassocks, monks' cowls or sandals, or nuns' habits. Muslims able to recognize their fellow believers will not think they are marked as inferior, whatever Lord Cromer thought of the veil. We do not hear of any movements to "liberate" Jews from the yarmulke. During civil rights demonstrations of the 1960s and 1970s, people wearing Roman collars were not necessarily priests of the Catholic, Episcopal, or Orthodox churches. Some Protestant pastors, black and white, wore them to express solidarity with their brothers in Christ (as Larycia Hawkins expressed solidarity with her Muslim sisters). Caner Dagli rightly says of verse 33.59:

> It is reasonable to assume that early jurists saw dress at least partly as a signifier of rank or communal identity . . . rather than solely in connection with indecency and temptation. (SQ 876)

The only other verse that concerns a Muslim woman's clothing is equally concerned with men's decorum.

> [Prophet], tell believing men to lower their eyes and guard their private parts: that is purer for them. God is well aware of everything they do. And tell believing women that they should lower their eyes, guard their private parts, and not display their charms beyond what [it is acceptable] to reveal; they should draw their coverings over their necklines and not reveal their charms except to their husbands, their fathers, their husbands' fathers, their sons, their husbands' sons, their brothers, their brothers' sons, their sisters' sons, their women-folk, their slaves, such men as attend them who have no desire [*eunuchs*], or children who are not yet aware of women's nakedness; they should not stamp their feet so as to draw attention to any hidden charms. Believers, all of you, turn to God so that you may prosper. (24.30–31)

Haleem translates *zina* as "charms." It can be rendered (according to SQ 876) as "decoration," or "embellishment," or "adornment," or "finery," or "something that beautifies." It is something added to a woman that enhances her attractiveness. One might think it is the naked body, since it can be shown to children, who have no knowledge of it, and to eunuchs, who have no interest in it, and to husbands, who have a right to it. But nakedness cannot normally be shown (as "charms" can) to close relatives or slave girls. It can be shown by dancing, which would seem to rule out forms of decoration, like jewels. Charm would seem more behavioral than a thing like a jewel—that is why it can be displayed by unlowered eyes or a way of dancing where that is appropriate—with husbands or intimates. These few references to decorum in clothing are superficial. But the "God consciousness" they manifest has deeper roots in Islamic theology.

NOTES

1. Leila Ahmed, *Women and Gender in Islam* (Yale University Press, 1992), p. 167.
2. A partial recent list: Leila Ahmed, Asma Barlas, Maria Massi Dakake, Riffat Hassan, Azizah al-Hibri, Fatema Mernissi, Amina Wadud. See Suha Taji-Farouki, ed., *Modern Muslim Intellectuals and the Qur'an* (Oxford University Press, 2004), pp. 97–124.
3. See Ahmed's chapter "The First Feminists" In *Women and Gender* (pp. 169–88), which treats women like these:

   Nabawiyya Musa (1886–1951)
   Huda Sha'rawi (1879–1947)
   Saiza Nabarawi (1897–1985)
   Malak Hifni Nasif (1886–1918)
   Doria Shafik (1908–1975)
   Zaynab al-Ghazali (1917–2005)

4. Edward. W. Said, *Orientalism*, 25th anniversary ed. (Vintage, 1994), p. 36.
5. Said quotes (p. 38) chapter 34 of Cromer's massive two-volume work, *Modern Egypt* (Macmillan, 1908), in which he quoted Sir Alfred Lyall: "'Accuracy is abhorrent to the Oriental mind. Every Anglo-Indian should always remember that maxim.' Want of accuracy, which easily degenerates into untruthfulness, is in fact the main characteristic of the Oriental mind."

6. Ahmed, op. cit., p. 151.

7. Ibid., pp. 152–53.

8. Ibid., p. 155.

9. James Gerstenzang and Lisa Getter, "Laura Bush Addresses State of Afghan Women," *Los Angeles Times,* Nov. 18, 2001.

10. Ahmed, op. cit., pp. 223–24.

Envoi: Fairness in Reading

R eading the Qur'an is not initially an easy task. But it is important, since second- and thirdhand reports on its contents are so
often selective and tendentious. What *is* easy is to sense the overall
tenor and priorities of the book. A few verses endlessly cited have
to do with violence. The grimmest are reserved for polytheists and
apostate Muslims. Some of those are cited and applied to Christians and Jews, against whom as such violence is never condoned.

The overall tenor is one of mercy and forgiveness, which are
evoked everywhere, almost obsessively. I am reminded of the few
verses of the New Testament that are unforgiving (again, directed
principally to pagans and apostates), as opposed to the nearly obses-
sive command to care for the poor, the weak, the neglected. When
Pope Francis says that Christians can learn from the Qur'an, he is
not saying that we will learn something absent from the New Testament, but that we will reveal our own deepest spiritual selves by
discovering the depths of other devotion. We recognize ourselves
in the true image of other believers, in the Qur'an or in the Torah.
We believers encourage each other over the barriers raised by people
who do not wish any of us well.

Index